SPARROW IN THE RAZOR WIRE

ADVANCE PRAISE

"Redemption is one of the most powerful forces on Earth. If you have doubts, Quan Huynh's courageous, brutally honest, and compelling memoir is some of the best evidence you'll find."

—Bryan Stevenson, executive director, Equal Justice Initiative and author of #1 *New York Times* bestseller, *Just Mercy*

"The first time I heard Quan speak, my jaw literally dropped. I could not believe his courage and vulnerability. I have only become more impressed with him as I've gotten to know him. His book is an incredible story of resilience, compassion, and hope from a man I am proud to call a friend. I can't recommend his story enough."

—Tucker Max, 4x *New York Times* bestselling author

"Quan's story illustrates a lifelong process of identity formation—from a child finding his place in the world, to a gang member trying to improve his social standing and self-respect, to a convicted murderer learning to thrive within the rules of prison culture, and finally to a curious and humble person working to improve his own life and the lives of others."

—Earlonne Woods, co-creator and co-host of the Pulitzer Prize Finalist podcast, *Ear Hustle*, and former life-term prisoner

"Quan's story illuminates that 'most of the time, what holds us back is entirely in our heads.' From the time he made the decision to transform his mindset and find freedom inside the walls of a prison, Quan demonstrated the kind of passion and persistence that allowed him to knock down the barriers to his future."

—Steve Sims, author of *Bluefishing*

"Quan's is a story of personal transformation that can give hope to those who are currently incarcerated, as well as to those who will one day be their neighbors."

—Chris Wilson, author of *The Master Plan* and former life-term prisoner

5 STAR AMAZON REVIEWS

"This book takes you inside prison and the mind of someone sentenced to a life term. You get a glimpse of what it's like to be incarcerated and some of the intense physical and mental struggles. Quan's story is authentic, heart-wrenching, and powerful. His stories of fellow inmates left me in tears and will stick in my mind forever. It's hard to believe what people can and are enduring everyday in the prison system, and yet still overcome. This book brings up the deepest and darkest parts of who we are as humans, and yet leaves you feeling inspired and hopeful."

—**Diana**, ★★★★★

"This is a powerful story of transformation and truth. Quan boldly lays it all on the table with regards to his journey. If you have ever looked at another person and made a judgment about them, read this book. I highly recommend it for anyone."

—**Mark**, ★★★★★

"As someone interested in the extremes of the human condition, I found Quan's narrative and life conveyed in this book very insightful. Written in a very real way, as if Quan was talking directly to you, just as he does with his numerous friends throughout the book. A deeper understanding of guilt, acceptance, love, pride and each of our natures is expressed in simple, but profound, terms. Rarely have I read such a raw portrayal of self, one that made me examine my own path of self-actualization. Highly recommend to anyone who has ever asked "why?" in response to injustice in our society."

—Aaron and Christina, ★★★★★

"Amidst one of the most difficult situations a human can face, the author finds redemption while in prison. This story is simultaneously heartbreaking, moving, entertaining, and overall, an important piece of art that everyone should read to get closer to understanding others, themselves, and the pursuit of true joy and fulfillment."

—Jacqueline, ★★★★★

"I have never read a more authentic and honest story. This book was so compelling because Quan told his story with raw truths. He helped the reader not only learn about his journey, but also view their own journey in a different and deeper way. Quan helps the reader recognize how redemption and taking responsibility for one's actions coincide. Reading his story made me want to look inside myself and think about what I need to improve. It made me want to take responsibility for my actions. It made me want to forgive. It made me want to humbly take correction from others and be my most authentic self."

—Aimee, ★★★★★

REVIEWS FROM THE INSIDE

"Thank you for the book. Your book and story gave me your perspective on board, and to continue focusing on transformation. Yes there will be bumps in the road, but it's how we know how to get over them correctly. I really liked your book a lot. In a way, I see this as help, reaching out to me in how to handle and go about my board the next time."

—Christopher, 29 years old, 11 years incarcerated

"I really enjoyed your book. I found it inspiring, uplifting, and informative. The greatest impact your book had on me was of hope. I see that the hard and uncomfortable work is going to pay off. Your book affirmed this to me. So I will persist until I succeed."

—Raul, 45 years old, 20 years incarcerated

"I was very moved and touched by your story that I couldn't put your book down. As I read your book, you started to give me insight into how I could approach my own board date. You painted a story, not just any story, but a story the world hasn't understood with clarity. You've given me a new view of my own self, as well as prison too. You have the spirit of a true fighter and a man of determination, you are a gift to many and I know one day we will cross paths."

—Ronald, 36 years old, 17 years incarceratedate

sparrow in the razor wire

Finding Freedom from Within While Serving a Life Sentence

QUAN HUYNH

SPARROW IN THE RAZOR WIRE
Finding Freedom from Within While Serving a Life Sentence

ISBN 978-1-5445-1441-3 *Hardcover*
978-1-5445-1440-6 *Paperback*
978-1-5445-1439-0 *Ebook*
978-1-5445-1442-0 *Audiobook*

For the men I left behind.

CONTENTS

FOREWORD

We all live in prisons.

I've traveled to eighty-five countries around the world, lived in some, worked in others, and witnessed deeply the human experience in all of them.

In the deep coaching and healing work I do—including my own journey—I see people often caught up and imprisoned by something. It may be our fears, our regrets, or the deeper unspoken shame that prevents an aliveness within us. Many of us are trapped by the past or entrapped by the patterns that appear to defy logic, yet still play out as if with a mind of their own.

Just when I am beginning to believe I have arrived at the gates of awareness, the universe throws something at me to remind me of how far I have to go and grow.

It felt as though Quan was one of those anomalies that was here to test me…and maybe you.

I met Quan at an event called Mastermind Talks. On the opening morning, we were intentionally sat together. I introduced myself to this sheepish-looking man. I was instantly struck by his energy. It wasn't bad, but something was off.

His eyes looked, for lack of a better term, unworthy.

For some deeper intuitive reason, I leaned over and said, "You know you belong here." He initially greeted my words with a degree of suspicion and then a teary-eyed acceptance. We started talking and connected at a soul level.

I've often prided myself on my ability to not judge people and to openly accept them for who they are and what they've done.

Not this day.

Later that morning, I found out that Quan was part of a rehabilitation program that helps previously incarcerated people assimilate back into society. They start by helping people develop on the inside years before their release, to prepare them to reenter a world that does not want them.

Then I found out why Quan was incarcerated for many years.

It was for murder.

My mind jumped to instant judgment, and my heart was overrun and silenced by the noise for a few minutes.

Then I remembered the eyes. Those eyes were the eyes of a good person. And the judgment began to subside.

Quan had stirred up something in me. A month later, I found myself traveling across the US to visit the maximum security prison Pelican Bay. Sitting in the car before I walked in the door, my mind started again with the questions and the judgments and the rationalizations. I had been invited to speak to a few hundred men, so I had to put my personal insecurities aside.

I tried to let them go and engage the men I met in prison as they came. The day was incredible. Yes, these men made mistakes. Yes, these men committed crimes (and some horrific crimes).

But there was goodness in them. Many of these men had owned their past, and I encouraged the rest to do the same. The ones who own their past did not once try and justify their actions. They took full responsibility for what they had done.

As the day unfolded, this "gap" between me and them eroded. At the end of the day, while I sat in my car and cried, it dawned on me: I had created this line, this gap, between who I am and who I thought they were.

It was a defensive stance to distance myself from them so I could tell myself that I am different.

The reality was, I was just like them. The only difference was my decisions. Those decisions that were deeply influenced by circumstances. I literally could have been any one of those men.

That truth scared the crap out of me and, at the same time, made me deeply grateful for the life I have.

We all have both light and darkness within us; and that day, that reality came home to me. When you deny the dark part of you, you also deny the light. And in the light is where your gift can emerge.

Months later, I was invited to bring the One Last Talk speaker series I founded into a prison in Colorado. The process helps you craft the last words you might speak into the world and the personal story you deep down need to share with the world. That day, six incarcerated men shared their One Last Talk behind bars to a live audience of other prisoners and members of the public. It was profound.

The men who delivered their One Last Talks that day fully accepted responsibility for all of their actions and choices. Most men and women behind bars have not. In fact, this is true for many people not behind bars as well.

But I believe that no person is beyond redemption. I believe that beginning with acceptance of responsibility and full ownership of one's life, anyone can move past their darkness and into the light of freedom—even if they are still behind the bars of a prison. To move past darkness, we must first step into it and bathe in its uncomfortableness.

Quan did not walk free the day he walked out the gates of prison. He began the walk to freedom years before, as a young man sitting in his cell. He stopped blaming the world and began to look inward at his own past and faced the darkness that influenced his decisions. He began the long internal journey to self-forgiveness and self-acceptance by doing just that: taking responsibility for what he had done.

No bars on earth can shackle a man who can access this in himself.

I wish, for humanity, that we could all begin this journey. The easy and socially accepted norm is to beat yourself up for the mistakes of the past. The courage it takes to begin that step, to really look in the mirror and accept what you have done, is remarkable.

This book and this story is not just for people in prison. It is for both the men and women around the world who sit behind metal bars and for those who walk the streets every day behind the invisible metal bars of their own self-imposed limitations.

I believe to my core that our greatest gifts lie right next to our deepest wounds.

Quan's gift is to help humanity free itself. He is deeply qualified to do so as he has experienced the pain of self- and literal imprisonment for most of his life.

I invited Quan to stand on a stage in Boulder and share his One Last Talk in front of a large audience. I got some kickback from some people in the audience beforehand for allowing a "murderer" to share his story. They judged me for letting him on stage before they'd even heard him.

His talk, "I Was Not Born This Way," was followed by a huge and instant standing ovation. One man took the mic to apologize for judging him before his talk.

That day, my nine-year-old son Charlie walked up to Quan after his talk (without any encouragement), hugged Quan, and said, "I loved your talk."

If a young boy can see beyond the mistakes he made, then maybe we all can too.

PHILIP MCKERNAN, FOUNDER OF ONE LAST TALK

"I have been all things unholy. If God can work through me, He can work through anyone."

—SAINT FRANCIS OF ASSISI

CHAPTER 1

LOST SOUL

PRESIDING COMMISSIONER: Now, once you caught up, then what happened?

INMATE HUYNH: When we caught up, I rolled down the window. And when the car came up onto the right of me, I pointed my gun, aimed at the car, and started shooting and unloaded the whole clip.

PRESIDING COMMISSIONER: What kind of gun was it?

INMATE HUYNH: It was a Sig Sauer nine-millimeter.

PRESIDING COMMISSIONER: Was it nine shots, twelve shots, what was it?

INMATE HUYNH: Fifteen shots.

On January 15, 1999, I shot and killed Minh Nguyen and tried to shoot and kill his three friends, David, Vincent, and Andrew. After our fight at a Hollywood nightclub, I put into effect a chain of events that would forever alter numerous lives. We followed them for about twenty miles before I did the shooting. To this day, I am still not sure why the fight started—because I wasn't there. It didn't matter to me, though; these guys had disrespected us by fighting my homeboys, so I wanted to shoot them.

I was twenty-four years old, attending college, and working at the Gallup Organization. This was before the fame of their Strengthsfinder studies, the personality assessment based on positive psychology that changed how the corporate world viewed management styles and talents. At that time, they were more known for their Gallup polls, and I was their 1998 Interviewer of the Year. Other managers suggested I interview for a management role. The position would have put me in charge of a location that had over 300 interviewers. Finally, for once in my life, it felt things would go right.

There was another side of my life, though. For the last seven years, I had been going in and out of juvenile hall and the California Youth Authority, where they housed the most serious juvenile offenders. I was released the previous year from a parole violation for possession of handguns and was still on active parole. I felt my life had no sense of purpose or direction.

On the one hand, I was a member of a violent and ruthless Vietnamese street gang, and on the other hand, I attended college and seemed on the outside to be as capable as the next person. I had no self-understanding of my true motives. I only knew that I wanted a better life than the one I was living but had no sense of where I could find it. The management position, and everything it represented, seemed to be the answer. Yet I was also seeking status, a form of success, in the gang life. Later, I would learn how wrong I was in pursuing either path. It would take a life sentence in prison for me to find true meaning and purpose in my life.

Several months after the interview, I was notified by the management team that I was not a fit. This news crushed me. I was ashamed and upset; I did not share the bad news with anyone. Instead, I stuffed it into a dark corner of my mind. That night, at the club in Hollywood, I felt agitated and restless. I wished I had been in the fight. I wanted to pull all the disappointment, anger, and hurt I felt about being turned down at Gallup and take it out on someone else. The rival gang members were from a gang out of Los Angeles, while we were from Orange County; but honestly, it did not matter.

Whenever something in my daily life frustrated or upset me, I found an outlet in the gang lifestyle. In the back of my mind, because I felt like a failure for not getting the management position at Gallup, I became more determined to succeed as a gang member.

In the gang life, I loved the sense of power that came from a gun, and all my homeboys knew I preferred the Sig Sauer handguns. The Sig Sauer had no safety and a hair trigger, and was to me, far superior to any other gun. It was similar to how I saw myself in regard to other gang members on the streets. This night, I had one with two high-capacity clips with fifteen rounds each and one extended clip with another thirty rounds. They always told me sixty shots was overkill; I disagreed. I had experienced enough of the gang lifestyle to keep a gun in my car at all times, along with enough bullets to be prepared for anything. I had been involved in numerous shootings, and in some of them, I ran out of bullets. It terrified me; I overcompensated by making sure I would always have more than enough.

We followed the four men from the rival gang for over twenty miles. They were in a red Honda Civic. We were waiting for the moment that the freeways would clear so there would be no witnesses to the shooting. I sat in the front right seat and had black cotton gloves on, smoking a cigarette while caressing my gun. My Sig Sauer had custom rubber Hogue grips on it; these are made to reduce recoil and provide better grip on a handgun. There was something oddly comforting in the contrast between the soft synthetic grips and the cold steel in my hands. The high-capacity clip and the extended clip rested in my lap.

We turned on a stretch of freeway, and I did not see any other cars either behind or in front of us. This was the moment. I had shot people before. The gun would erupt, my ears would ring, and the smell of gunpowder would permeate the car. But I had yet to kill someone and wanted to be successful tonight. I rolled down my window and flicked out the cigarette. I fleetingly saw the embers bounce on the highway behind us, and I told the driver of my car to pass the Honda on their left. The wind was already rushing in my ears. I aimed my gun through the tritium night sights at the back rear window. The only one I was concerned with was the left rear passenger; he would be the only one who could shoot at us as we came alongside them. His window was rolled up, which told me they had no idea what was coming.

Our car was going over ninety miles per hour when we sped by, and I started unloading at his profile, very similar to the hundreds of paper silhouettes I shot at inside gun ranges. Their car swerved to the right, and I continued to shoot at the rest of the occupants in the vehicle until the clip was empty. I ejected the cartridge and slammed in the extended clip, then looked back toward the red Civic. I hoped they would chase us, thinking I was out of bullets. We could have a real gun battle, and I would have a nice surprise for them. Instead, they pulled over.

The wind was still rushing in through the open window, and it did nothing to remove the smell of gunpowder in the car. My ears were ringing, and my heart was beating triumphantly. Nothing had me feeling more alive than these moments did. It was life or death. The sense of excitement after every shooting made everything else in my life feel dull in comparison. Yet, it was only temporary until my next shooting. I looked for shell casings in my front seat, lap, and side door panel. Expended shell casings always ended up in the weirdest places in a car, and I definitely did not want any of them to ever be found as evidence after a shooting. I instructed the other passengers in my car to look for them on the backseat and floor. We found one that had somehow wedged underneath where I sat, so I wiped it down with my gloves to remove any trace of fingerprints, then flicked it out the window. I lit up a cigarette, and we drove home in silence.

When I got home, I walked into my mother's room to check on her, as was my ritual. She had this habit of waking up in the middle of the night whenever I went out, and I felt the need to let her know I was home safe. This night, she was sleeping and had kicked the covers off. I pulled the blankets back up and gave her a gentle kiss on the forehead. She mumbled something and fell back asleep. She looked so peaceful with the light of the moon on her face. I yearned to feel that way inside.

The next day, I found out that one person died and a couple of others were injured in the shooting. I broke down my gun into different pieces and threw the parts away in random places throughout Orange County. I threw one piece in the Dumpster and another in the ocean from the edge of the pier. Late one night, I buried the barrel in a new construction site near my house before they poured in the concrete. In effect, I made the murder weapon disappear forever. The only thing I kept was the Hogue grips for the next Sig Sauer I planned to find through my connections on the streets. I washed the gloves to remove any trace of gunpowder residue and then put them back in my car. I thoroughly went through my car one last time and vacuumed it all up, wiped the whole interior down, then went back to my day-to-day living.

Nobody outside the occupants in my car knew I had just murdered another human being, and I felt I carried the darkest of all secrets. At home, I still carried on the same conversations with my family. I showed up to work and school, and everyone treated me the same. But the world was not the same. The same food that I always enjoyed tasted bland. The same conversations with friends and family now felt disconnected. I had entertained thoughts of killing people multiple times, but now that it finally happened, I felt a need to go back to church.

That Sunday, I stepped into Mass and looked up at the crucifix hanging up near the rafters of the church. The organ music was playing and people were singing. I hoped to experience something when Mass started but only felt the same emptiness inside. *There is no such thing as God.* It was something I suspected more than ten years ago when my father died. Yet, I never had the courage to admit it to myself. The parishioners began to line up to receive communion, and I walked out in disgust. *Why would these people pray to a god that did not exist?* They were all pathetic.

Meanwhile, Los Angeles County Sheriff's detectives and Orange County gang detectives discovered that our gang was responsible for the shooting. Several months after the murder, I was taken into custody under a gang sweep, and one of my homeboys turned state's evidence and snitched on me. I was first tried for the death penalty, then the state decided my case would be tried for life without the possibility of parole. My homeboy ended up getting on the stand to testify against me and was the state's only evidence. Everyone else on the case pled the Fifth and refused to cooperate with the police. My attorney and I decided the only way to refute his testimony was for me to get on the stand myself. I lied on the stand and said I was only in the backseat of the car and blamed the snitch for doing the shooting. I was ultimately found guilty of second-degree murder under the felony murder rule. The jury believed I was not the shooter. All other enhancements, including gun charges, were found to be not true. I was pissed because I almost got away with it all. I was sentenced to fifteen years to life.

At the time, a life sentence in the state of California was the same as a death sentence because *nobody* was ever paroled, whether it was a five-to-life or fifty-to-life sentence. I was sent off to one of the prison reception centers in Delano to do an intake interview with the correctional counselors.

In the reception centers, we were locked in our cells twenty-three hours a day. One hour was for recreational yard and shower. I usually stood at my cell door and looked out over the dayroom to observe what was going on because of boredom, doing sets of push-ups in between. Men would be called out for ducats, prison lingo for passes, to go see medical staff or meet their counselors for intake interviews. Typically, intake interviews with counselors were done in closed offices. For some reason, my correctional counselor decided to do our intake interview in the dayroom with other prisoners watching. She smelled of stale cigarettes, looked disinterested in her work, and repeatedly pronounced my last name wrong after I had corrected her several times. She was going through my case factors to determine what prison I would be housed at and my security level.

In the California prisons, the higher the points, the higher the security level. My probation report stated I was a gang member, and the counselor asked me to sign a document admitting to it. Admitting to being a gang member would give me additional points. Of course, I refused, and she became upset. She then proceeded to add points to my case factors because she said she had no record of a high school diploma or employment in my file. It did not make sense because the same probation report stated I was in college and had a job. It was obvious she was picking and choosing what she wanted from the probation report to give me as many points as possible. She then tried to slide the gang documentation paper to me again.

I looked at her and said, "Let me ask you something. You keep referencing my probation report to give me points for being a gang member, and if you are going to use that, then you should also give me credit for employment and a high school diploma. I shouldn't be penalized for not having that when it clearly states in my probation report I was working and in college at the time."

She rolled her eyes and looked right past me. This infuriated me further. I lost it and said, "Are you sure that you even got a high school diploma yourself when you applied for this job?" The other prisoners in the dayroom started giggling, and the counselor glared at me and closed the file folder.

"We're done here," she stated and shuffled out of the dayroom.

Within a few days, I received notice that I was going to Pelican

Bay, a notorious prison home to the most violent and high-profile gang members. For me at the time, getting sent to the Bay, as it was known, was another badge of honor. The other prisoners in reception told me I was sent there because I had told off the correctional counselor during the intake interview. I did not care.

Pelican Bay is situated on the northern tip of California, several miles from the Oregon border. The bus ride took over two days, as we had to lay over at a couple of prisons to drop off and pick up other prisoners. Each of us were in waist and leg shackles. We were instructed to not talk, but of course, since we all had life sentences, the men did not care. One man in particular refused to listen to the correctional officers after repeated warnings, until they stopped the bus, dragged him out, and beat him with their batons. It angered me that they were in positions of authority, yet inflicted violence on helpless individuals. I justified that at least the people I harmed could fight back. These correctional officers were cowards in my eyes.

After that, the whole bus ride was completely silent. We drove through the most beautiful redwood forests and along the edge of the California coast. On the second night, we pulled up to the Bay, and there was a sergeant waiting for us with several other correctional officers standing around. They ordered us off and lined us up in front of the bus.

He looked at us and then said, "On behalf of my family, I want to thank each and every one of you. I don't care what you did; I only care that you are here now." He smiled and continued looking at each of us. "You will all be here for the rest of your lives, and you have provided a way for me and my men here to take care of our families. For that, I want to thank you from the bottom of my heart." I was hungry and tired, but this insult upset me further. I wished I could shoot him in the face. They all snickered and shuffled us into the prison for intake. None of us said anything, and we became the newest prisoners at Pelican Bay.

The prison was on a modified lockdown, as some of the prisoners had plotted an attack on the correctional officers, and we only came out of our cells to go eat in the chow hall. Inside the chow hall, there was an officer right above us holding a Mini-14 rifle on a catwalk. A large sign on the wall read, "No Warning Shots." Each time I went to eat, I shoveled food into my mouth while continuing to look all around me. If a fight broke out, I wanted to be able to protect myself from both the assailant and the officer up above who would be shooting down at us. I hated the chow hall; the food was overcooked and I felt defenseless. But hunger, and a fear of what other people would think of me if I did not show up, drove me to go each day.

Early one morning, less than a year later, I turned on the TV in my cell to watch the news and saw a building on fire at the World Trade Center in New York City. My cellmate was still sleeping, and nobody on the news knew what was going on. As I watched, I saw a second plane crash into the other tower, followed by a large explosion.

We were in a place that seemed eternally frozen in time, yet the actions of the 9/11 terrorists affected even the prisoners of Pelican Bay. The prison locked us all down for what they called safety and security reasons. The usual banter among the prisoners behind their locked cell doors was unusually quiet, and as I lay in bed, restless and bored, I realized this is what my life might be like until the day I died.

CHAPTER 2

CONVERSATIONS WITH MY FATHER

PRESIDING COMMISSIONER: Mr. Huynh, you were born in Vietnam?

INMATE HUYNH: Yes, sir.

PRESIDING COMMISSIONER: And three months old, you relocated to Provo, Utah?

INMATE HUYNH: Yes, sir.

PRESIDING COMMISSIONER: So you grew up primarily as a teenager, was it Utah or California?

INMATE HUYNH: As a teenager, in California. We left Utah when I was ten years old when my father's condition started deteriorating from leukemia. And we moved here to California because his side of the family is here in California.

I was not born a murderer.

My earliest memory of anger and shame goes back to when I was eight years old. It was a hot summer in Provo, Utah. The snow melt had filled the ditches with fresh stream water. My younger brother and I would build rafts out of Popsicle sticks and float our GI Joe action figures down imaginary river rapids. We chased the rafts downstream in flip-flops and shorts, icy water almost up to our knees. It was a welcome relief from the hot sun beating down on us.

Some older kids and what looked like adults were on a fence at the top of the ditch. They began throwing rocks down at us, and one of them yelled, "Go back to your country!" This was not the first time we were teased for our race. This day, though, we felt brave because the fence was high and they seemed so far away.

"Come and make us!" we yelled back.

They jumped the fence and made their way down one side of the ditch. We grabbed our action figures and homemade rafts and clambered up the other side. The adults at the fence began cheering, and we ran as fast as possible. Somewhere along the way, I dropped my action figures and stopped to pick them up. My younger brother turned to face our aggressors, and they pushed him to the ground. He tried to fight back until one of the older kids punched him in the face, and he rolled over. They held his face to the ground and shoved dirt in his mouth. In between choking and crying, he looked up at me for help.

I stood in fear and did nothing.

We both walked home crying, our faces covered in dust, broken up by the tracks of our tears. When my father found out what happened, he looked at me in his quiet way. "How could you let this happen to your younger brother? You are supposed to protect your family." I felt ashamed that I had let my family down.

Later that summer, I was in the sandbox at my elementary school with a couple of other kids playing. I had taken off my shoes to play in the sand and tied them around the handlebars on my bike. Another kid with blond curly locks began playing with us, too. Somewhere during our back-and-forth banter as children, he stated that my family ate grasshoppers. I went into a rage and punched and kicked him. He fought back, and I fell down with him straddling me. He began to choke me until I hooked both my feet around his face and chest and forced him backward. His head hit one of the metal poles of the swings, and he fell over and began to cry.

I did not stop there. There was so much humiliation I felt after the incident with my brother. My father never said anything about it again, which made things worse in my mind. I already promised myself the next time somebody insulted my family, I would fight them to the end. Whatever the end was.

The kid had curled up outside the sandbox. I sat on top of him, grabbed his hair, and slammed his head and face into the concrete. The more he screamed, the harder I tugged and shoved his face into the ground. Tufts of his hair came loose in my hands and I gripped more of it. I felt an exhilarating sense of power as I was doing it and did not want to let go. The other kids in the sandbox stood in silence. When I heard the voice of an adult, I got up and rode away. As I pedaled my bike, one of the shoes I had tied on the handlebars came off, and I turned back for it. I knew my father would yell at me for losing my shoe. That is when the adult grabbed me.

"Look at what you have done to my son!" he screamed at me.

His son's face was already swelling up, and there was blood over his nose and mouth. I was terrified and began to cry. The kid's long yellow locks were now stuck and matted to his head. "Why did you do this?" the dad asked.

"Because he said we eat grasshoppers." I wept.

The dad turned to his son. "Did you say this?"

The son nodded. The dad sat us down and began to share that his family grew up so poor they gathered dandelions to eat as kids. He turned to his son and stated that he should never say anything about another family.

I wish all my experiences with ignorance, bigotry, and racism ended with such valuable learning lessons as this. At school, we were the only Vietnamese family for quite a while. Everywhere we went it seemed people would look at us, point, laugh, and whisper. Our house was decorated with toilet paper a few times. Religion played such a great social factor in Utah, and we were subtly, but not maliciously, treated as outsiders. Utah is predominantly Mormon, whereas my family is Roman Catholic.

Of course, I have come to understand these were mostly isolated incidents, and the vast majority of people in Utah are kind and warm-hearted. But these events led me to believe there was something different about me and my family, that we were outcasts. I only wished we could be like everyone else.

Luckily, I had my father to turn to during these times of doubt. I could always go to him and ask him questions and he had all the answers. He made everything all right. He was a kind and gentle man. His first job in our new country was as a custodian during the graveyard shift at the local supermarket. With savings from his first few paychecks, he bought himself a bike so he would not have to walk to work. As a young boy growing up, my father was my hero, and I believed he was invincible. I recall numerous stories of how he had attended the Vietnamese Military Academy. There were many old black-and-white photographs of him in his officer's uniform. My fondest memories of my father were his morning car rides to neighboring states. Early one Saturday morning before dawn, I happened to wake up and see my father getting dressed. He was pulling on his familiar green military jacket that he wore everywhere.

"Where you going, Dad?"

"I have some business to take care of this morning," he whispered. He straightened his jacket, then looked down at me. "Do you want to go?"

I nodded.

We left early when it was still pitch black. While on the highway, I witnessed the early light of morning, when the darkness began to lighten up with faint hues of purple. I began to make out the familiar silhouette of the Rocky Mountains. I did not blink, and I did not breathe. The moment was magical, and I got to experience this beauty in the company of my father. We both stayed quiet and soaked it all in.

From that day forth, on our trips, I always tried to not blink when the sun was rising so I could catch the exact moment when the first rays of light would separate from the darkness. Then I would close my eyes and sleep until we got to wherever we were going that morning. My father drove to neighboring states to help fill out the DMV or Social Security paperwork for other Vietnamese families.

This seemed boring, and I did not understand why my father would drive all that way to do paperwork for people he did not even know, especially since he was not getting paid for it. He told me something about helping people in the community, but I could not grasp the significance of what he was teaching me at the time. What I did enjoy was his company, though, just the two of us. These early morning business trips of his would take all day, and we would get home late in the evening, tired and hungry. Of course, my mother would have something hot and delicious waiting for us on the dinner table. Our family would all eat together. It became a ritual that I accompanied my father on these business trips of his on the weekends to help out our community. These trips with my father are the strongest memories I have of feeling loved and safe as a child.

On these road trips, I also had all my life's questions answered. One of my biggest dilemmas growing up was why my peers were so much bigger than I was. In my elementary years, I was smaller than kids my age because I was born premature. I asked my father about it. He had all the answers. My father explained that I was actually blessed because being smaller meant that my brain would not have to pump as much blood throughout my body. This in turn would make me smarter than my peers.

Problem solved.

During the '80s, martial arts shows were popular on television. Bruce Lee was one of my heroes. One day, I noticed that the actors had a funny way of talking. The majority of martial arts movies were dubbed, but as a young child, I did not understand that. All I knew was the mouths of the actors moved weird when they spoke. I was horrified as I realized that I must have looked like that when I talked! This explained why kids made fun of me at school. I got in front of the mirror after the kung fu show and began mouthing out words.

"Hello. How are you? What are you doing?" I said to myself, paying particular attention to how my mouth moved. I still could not figure out this mystery until I brought it up with my father on an early morning ride. My father laughed in that gentle way of his and explained to me how English words were dubbed. He told me the reason the kids made fun of me at school was because they did not understand us and that I should learn to be proud of our culture. This in my mind did not exactly add up because I wanted to be normal like the other kids, but I accepted it because my father knew everything.

My father was involved in political activism for displaced Vietnamese communities. Sometime in the '80s, he founded the Vietnamese Refugee Association. They coordinated many of our cultural celebrations in which Vietnamese communities throughout the neighboring states would come together to celebrate. My father was constantly on the local television newscasts and in the newspapers, which only made him more superhuman in my eyes. Because of his political connections, we soon had politicians at our house for dinner several times a week. These politicians told me that when I grew up, I should attend the United States Military Academy at West Point so I could be like my father. These politicians encouraged me, from a young age, to be the first Vietnamese American to enter the academy. This was perfect because I wanted to be just like who I thought was the most extraordinary person in my life—my father.

My mother, on the other hand, is a stoic woman. There always seemed to be an emotional disconnection between us. Compared with families in my neighborhood and on television shows, my mother always seemed unhappy. Her words usually felt harsh, although they were not unkind or demeaning in any way. She constantly stressed the importance of attaining an education but seemed to dismiss our needs to be children and go outside and play. My mother placed tremendous importance on our family image and reputation. Everything was about what other families might think about us. I was expected to get good grades, attend Mass, and be a good kid. It never seemed I could measure up to her standards.

My mother did express her love, though, through cooking. She is an amazing cook. She has an amusing habit of standing and watching the family eat, preening with a sense of satisfaction while everyone wolfs down her food. She never said she loved me, but I do remember feeling loved whenever I sat down to eat one of her delicious meals.

My younger brother was my best friend. Being only a year and some odd months apart, we were constant companions. According to family lore, my brother was always bigger because he was born in America, while I was born premature in Vietnam. But our culture elevated me above him because I was the firstborn child. Therefore, not only did I have a bigger companion to accompany me wherever I went, but I also had somebody who would listen to whatever I commanded. This family dynamic instilled in me a lot of the entitlement and arrogance issues I struggle with to this day. At the time, though, I just thought it was normal for me to tell my brother what to do. Most of the time, the commands came in the form of me telling him to catch bugs and hold them up close so I could examine them. My brother was fearless. He would grab bumblebees, caterpillars with lethal-looking spikes on them, or whatever other insects seemed to catch my attention that day. We would cut orange wedges and shove them into our mouths as mouth guards and slugged out fight scenes from the movie *Rocky*. We also loved football and endlessly played against each other in the living room. I would represent the Dallas Cowboys, and his team was the Washington Redskins.

Now, if my younger brother was my foot soldier, our youngest sister was our personal slave. She happened to be born last into a family of two older brothers who had to exercise their sense of power. She was at the bottom of the pecking order. We ordered her to grab frozen chocolate Charleston Chew bars from the freezer when we were engrossed in our Atari video games. She was expected to refresh us with ice-cold Popsicles when we came back from battle in the backyard. We called her from our room while she was playing with her stuffed animals to hand her empty cereal bowls to put in the sink. My father took a picture that perfectly summed up our childhood. In it, my brother and I have our arms around our baby sister and smiling, while she is crying and sitting on the toilet. Even in her most intimate moments, we terrorized her.

During this time, my father was diagnosed with leukemia and hospitalized. Up to this point in my life, everything at home still seemed all right because I could always turn to my father if something went wrong. But to hear that my father had cancer and might die scared me. He was the foundation of our family and the center of my universe. Of course, I did not believe that my father could ever actually die, but for him to even get sick was quite frightening. If something were to ever happen to him, whom could I turn to for my life's questions? How could we ever catch the first sunrise again on our trips?

My father worked at the coal mines in a neighboring city when a tunnel collapsed. It was all over the news. He escaped unscathed; some rocks had fallen on his shoulder, but he went back to work within the week. Then, many of his coworkers were also diagnosed with cancer. There was some type of class action lawsuit against the government, alleging a connection between the diagnoses and underground nuclear testing. The lawsuit was later dismissed, but that was one of the reasons given for how my father might have developed leukemia. Five years later, he died.

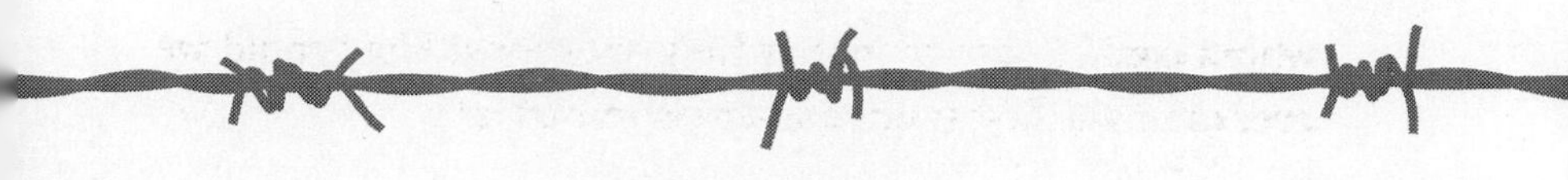

CHAPTER 3

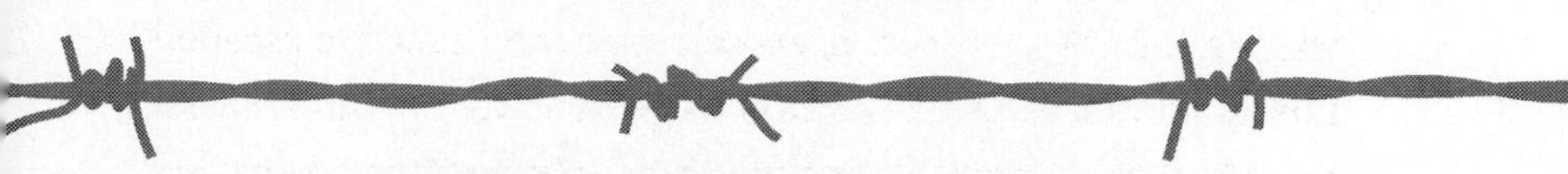

BETRAYAL OF MY FATHER

PRESIDING COMMISSIONER: And when you were ten years old, your family moved to California to be closer to the—your dad's family, and then your dad passed away on May the 8th, 1988, correct?

INMATE HUYNH: Yes.

PRESIDING COMMISSIONER: And at that time, how old were you when—

INMATE HUYNH: I was thirteen.

PRESIDING COMMISSIONER: Thirteen?

INMATE HUYNH: Yeah, that was also Mother's Day, and it was also the day of my First Communion, too.

When I was ten, my family moved to Santa Barbara, California, to be closer to my father's side of the family while he went through cancer treatment, and we eventually settled in Orange

County. California was a completely different world to me than Utah. The kids at school were not 99 percent white; now I went to class with Hispanic and Vietnamese kids, too. Maybe now I would find acceptance.

I remember one of the first conversations I had at my new school. I was climbing on the monkey bars and another kid came up to me. He asked me in Vietnamese if I was Vietnamese.

"Yes," I said.

"How old are you?" he asked.

"Eleven," I responded.

"But what is your Vietnamese age?" I had never been asked anything like that before and repeated I was eleven. He told me he was fourteen. I was confused. Wasn't he too old to be in sixth grade with me? That evening, my mother explained to me that some immigrant families falsified the ages of their children so they could go back several grade levels and learn English.

These kids were more mature than I was, both physically and emotionally, and many teased me for not speaking Vietnamese too well and for being whitewashed. I felt stuck between two cultures. I even found myself missing Utah. I do not know what it was exactly, but it felt like there was something about me that did not fit in. The white kids in Utah did not accept me, and now the Vietnamese kids did not either. There was something wrong with me.

On the home front, my father's cancer would go into remission and then come back again. Over the next several years, my father went in and out of the hospital. Whenever he was in the hospital, we went to Mass and prayed for him. During this time, I was confused toward my faith. When he was home, we were all happy as a family. When he was back in the hospital, I somehow believed I was to blame in some way, like God was punishing me for not being a good kid. I did not like attending Mass every week, and I believed God could see my heart and knew I was a bad kid.

By the age of twelve, my only escape from that loneliness was in books. I enjoyed reading fantasy novels and wished I could be a hero who could find a magic potion to save my father. Reading books helped to refine my writing skills, and in junior high I was recognized for my creative writing ability. My school funded me to take a creative writing workshop for the summer at the University of California in Irvine. Through writing, I found a channel to vent a lot of unexpressed emotions that I held on to inside. My family was proud of me, too.

The majority of the other kids in the summer course were from upper-class neighborhoods in Orange County. Their parents would drop them off and pick them up in Mercedes and BMWs. I was the kid from the lower income side of the county who took a public bus there. I was ashamed and walked to the far side of the campus so nobody would see me getting on or off a bus. In all, my commute to the writing workshop was over two hours each way.

My father's condition deteriorated, and he was in for an extended stay at the hospital. I was, of course, expected to visit him after the workshop. My days were spent writing, taking buses, and then going to the hospital. Meanwhile, the other kids from school and in my apartment building were enjoying their endless free time playing football and other games. I felt I was missing out and grew to resent my dad and hate the workshop. I became bitter at the novelty of being recognized for writing. There were no benefits to this gift. Little did I know, that summer would be the last time I would be involved in any creative writing classes until I was serving a life sentence in prison.

My mother was constantly depressed about my father's condition. She spoke about how hopeless it all seemed. This in turn made me feel even more powerless because I wanted to help her. I thought, as the oldest son, I was expected to be the hero and savior. I was failing and did not know what to do. Since my father never expressed any fears, I came to believe that men who expressed any type of emotion were weak. I definitely did not want to feel weak. That inability to express emotions, though, made me feel even more isolated.

The hospital visits with my father became unbearable for me over the next year. He was dying before my eyes. I resented that the situation made me feel sad, scared, and weak. Instead, I looked for a reason to argue and pick a fight with my father, then I would have a legitimate excuse to not see him for a few days. But then I would feel guilty. My prayers were going unanswered, and my sense of shame and resentment toward both God and my father was building.

One evening after Mass, my mom drove us to the hospital. As we pulled up in the parking lot, she began to sob and said that my father did not have much time to live. It was one of the few times I saw her crying. She said there would be a priest there that night to do his last rites. When I stepped into my father's room, he looked even more sickly, his skin an unnatural pale yellow. A priest was standing there whispering to him.

The priest turned to our family and greeted us. A while later, he pulled out a thin black Bible and began reciting various prayers. Each of us began crying, including my father. I felt helpless and alone and sent out a pleading last prayer to God. *Please let me save him somehow!* Our First Communion was coming up, a pretty big deal in the church. I told myself I would be able to rescue my father by praying for him after I ate the communion for the first time. God definitely would have to grant my prayer that day.

That year, Mother's Day fell on the same day as our First Communion. I walked into the bathroom that morning to brush my teeth, and my younger sister poked her head out from behind the shower curtain. She looked at me and whispered, "Dad died last night," with huge pools of tears in her eyes. I was in shock. "I heard Mom and Grandma whispering about it last night. I don't think we're supposed to know."

We did not hug or console each other, and I did not respond to her. I shuffled back into the room that I shared with my brother and let him know the news. He grunted and then acted like he did not hear me. I heard my mother and paternal grandmother in the background whispering.

I put on an ill-fitting suit and a red clip-on tie and acted as normal as possible. The suit felt stiff and hot. My sister was in a pretty white dress, but I did not compliment her. We got into our mom's Honda Civic, my grandmother in the front, the three of us squeezed in the back. We referred to it as the Silver Bullet. It was so old that when we were all in it, the car would struggle going uphill. As it chugged along, nobody said anything. It was such an uncomfortable silence. It became stuffy, so I rolled the window down, but the fresh air did not help. We walked into church, and I saw all the kids around me at Mass had smiles, their parents filled with joy. I noticed many parents had their arms around their children. Nobody hugged us. Everything felt numb inside.

I stood there in Mass with my head down. I could not cry because it would let my family know we overheard them about my father's death. I could not cry because that meant I was weak. I could not cry because I could not accept my father was dead. The priest was rambling that day about how much we were blessed to be able to have family there and to be part of this celebration.

Rather than comfort me, these words upset me. God had killed my father so that He would not have to grant my prayer that day. God did not grant my prayer because I was undeserving and there was something fundamentally wrong with me as a person and a son. I knew that I had failed. Everything up to that point in my life confirmed it. There was so much emptiness inside.

Next, we lined up to receive communion. I walked up to the priest as he held up the bread and said, "The body of Christ." I felt sick to my stomach as it was placed on my tongue. The wafer stuck to the roof of my mouth. When we walked out to the parking lot, my mother told us that our father had passed away the night before. My sister started throwing up. My grandmother mumbled something to the effect that my father was in a better place. I blocked everything out, numb with disbelief.

In our culture, immediate family members wear a white cloth wrapped around their heads at a funeral, so other guests can give their condolences.

My father's funeral was a blur. Many of the families that he helped throughout the years showed up. I met a few men who had attended the military academy with him. They all commented that I was a strong boy because I was not crying. I felt weak inside but definitely did not want anyone to ever know. I watched everyone and noticed only the women cried. *This is what it means to be a man*, I realized. *Never show emotions, do not express them, and do not, whatever you do, cry.* I do not remember hugging my brother, sister, or mom after my father's death, or being asked how I was feeling, or anything. I was in a lonely little shell.

Why would the God I prayed to every Sunday not grant the only thing I ever asked for? I felt guilty for the many times I did not visit my father when I walked home from school. I regretted every argument and subsequent temper tantrum I threw to not spend time with him at the hospital. I had said such harsh words to him on some days, and now he was dead. Now the guilt of that betrayal further supported my belief of being flawed. My father's death put my mother in a deep depression. She expressed her despair by constantly saying things that made me feel I was not a good enough son in her eyes. When I came home from school without straight As, she reminded me that my father would be disappointed in me. I needed good grades so I could get to West Point, so I could not let him down. One day, we were at a Taco Bell restaurant. While waiting for our order, she said she wished I was old enough to work so I could help out with the family finances. I felt helpless, and my animosity toward her grew. My father had always been disappointed in me, and I had never been able to help my family with anything.

At my father's funeral, each family member was given a small square piece of white cloth, the size of a quarter. We pinned it to our clothes, and it signified we were mourning the death of a loved one. One of my first days in high school, someone asked the meaning of the cloth. I explained, and he gave me a weird look and walked off. It happened a few more times with other kids, too. It felt that I should be over the death of my father, and I was looking for sympathy in some way. I felt so self-conscious that one day, I went into the boy's restroom and flushed the cloth down the toilet. I choked back tears as it spiraled down the toilet bowl. I did not want to stand out. I did not want to be weak over my father's death. My mom noticed and commented that I must be done grieving. I definitely was not. The irony was, I had not even begun yet. It became a symbol of defiance to not wear it, that I was not weak, and there was nothing wrong with me. Yet, I felt I was further betraying my father's memory by not having the mourning cloth on me. It was a destructive cycle of guilt and shame. I was betraying the memory of my father but was too ashamed to let the world know that his death hurt terribly. I was angry with God and hated showing up to Mass each week with my mom and siblings, each of us withdrawn in a shell of silence. Detaching from the world and my faith was the easier choice to make. Twenty-five years later, I realized it was these series of disconnections that had made me capable of murder.

CHAPTER 4

SEARCH FOR MEANING

PRESIDING COMMISSIONER: What was the 1991 arrest for?

INMATE HUYNH: The arrest was for three attempted murders of some skinhead youths at my school. They went to school with me and my brother.

PRESIDING COMMISSIONER: Did you do well there in terms of adjustment?

INMATE HUYNH: Well, I don't know if that would be adjusting because I think that's where I conformed and I took up a lot of the gang values that I later brought out to the streets. I adopted a lot of the warped way that they thought, that they were thinking, and I carried that with me to streets...but I wouldn't say I adjusted well because that's where I think my criminality deepened.

By the time I was a senior in high school, I could feel the mounting pressures of my future looming. Other kids in high school already had acceptance letters to other colleges and knew where they wanted to go. I applied to a couple of colleges but knew I did not want to attend any of them.

My father wanted me to attend West Point, and even after his death I hoped to both honor him and redeem myself in some way. The previous summer, I had failed my SAT exams and knew there was no way I would be going to the academy. Yet, I did not share it with my mom. Instead, I filled out an application to the Reserve Officer Training Corps. Something about joining the military was much more attractive than going to college for me. One day, the recruiting officer called my house, and my mom picked up the phone.

"No, we are not interested. My son is not doing that. Don't call here anymore." She hung up the phone, then turned and looked at me. "Why are these recruiters calling our house for? Don't they know you are going to West Point?" Without waiting for an answer, she went back to bustling around in the kitchen.

I said nothing and acted like I did not hear her.

At the time, I was working at Subway, the sandwich shop. One evening, my brother and a couple of my friends came into my work. He looked upset and had a scowl on his face.

"Gumby and his friends just called our house and threatened our family." He sat down with my friends, and I came from around the counter. "They called the house, and said they were going to come in and kill Mom and everyone. I wish we had beat his ass worse last time at the beach."

Gumby was a self-proclaimed skinhead who attended a nearby continuation school. He had been arrested with stolen property and let the police know he got it from my brother. We ran into him at a beach party one night with what looked like a dozen other skinheads. I was with my brother and two of our friends, Ant and Red. My brother wanted to beat him up for snitching. As we approached Gumby, I stayed quiet. We were outnumbered, and fights made me nervous, unlike my brother. He thrived on the adrenaline of it and called Gumby out to fight. That night, Red had a .22 caliber handgun. He pulled it out and announced if anyone jumped in he would use it. I felt a new sense of courage as my brother dropped Gumby with an uppercut, and the skinheads stood back in fear. My friends roared victoriously as they jumped in, swarming on Gumby with their fists and feet. I joined my comrades in the fray, sucked in by the violence. Gumby ended up with broken ribs.

I felt fearful before the fight, but with the sense of power from our gun and the adrenaline of my brother fighting, I found myself looking forward to the next time we could hurt someone as a group.

Two nights after we jumped Gumby, a man and woman walked into my work right before closing time. They were wearing leather motorcycle jackets and I could make out tattoos on the man's wrists. He wore sunglasses and had a grim look. I suddenly felt nervous.

The woman began to speak. "I am Gumby's mom. We are here to make sure there are no other issues with my son." I kept my eye on the man and could tell he was trying to see if there was anyone else working in the store with me.

I took a step back from behind the counter, terrified inside. "Gumby told on my friends. There are no other issues as long as he does not say anything else."

"Gumby will not be talking to the police anymore. Just make sure you and your friends leave him alone. If something else happens to my son, we will be back." They walked out, and the word later in the streets was they had come in with a gun to shoot me. I am not sure why they thought I was the ringleader, but I found I liked being recognized like that.

This night at the Subway shop, Red was with my brother and had his .22 caliber gun with him. "Do you know where Gumby lives?" he asked. I didn't, but my coworker knew Gumby, and I convinced her to draw me a map of where he lived. I handed it to my brother and friends.

"OK, we'll be back to pick you up tonight after work, and we will go and shoot up his house," they said.

They never came to pick me up. Instead, they found someone else at a nearby arcade and he brought them to Gumby's house. Red ended up shooting three people inside. We were arrested within a couple of weeks, and they charged me with conspiracy to commit murder. Even though I was not at the scene of the crime, I was arrested because my coworker had drawn the map and given it to me. It did not matter if my friends used it or not.

Juvenile hall was terrifying. A large Samoan staff member told me to remove all my clothes, and I stood there completely naked. He then had me bend over and spread open my butt cheeks so he could look inside my rectum. It was humiliating. I stepped on a cold scale and weighed in at 106 pounds.

Juvenile hall reinforced to me, though, that as long as I victimized others, I would not be victimized. After one of the earliest visits with our mother, another kid, named Maples, kept staring at me and my brother. His face was scrunched up like someone had farted. He looked at us and said, "Are you guys Korean?"

"No, we're Vietnamese," I said.

He said, "I don't like Koreans, Vietnamese, Chinese, or whatever you guys are." Another Asian kid nearby heard and spit on Maples's face.

Maples did not even blink or flinch. A big loogie was making its way down his face. He stood up and slowly walked up to one of the juvenile hall staff. "Do you see this right here?" He pointed at his face. "Do you see this?"

The staff looked up and did a double take. "Looks like someone spit on your face, young man. Who did it?"

Maples turned and, with a smirk, pointed out the person who spit on him. "That gentleman right over there." He then took the bottom of his shirt and wiped off the spit and gave everyone a smile.

From that day forth, Maples was targeted. He had broken the code, and we all knew "snitches got stitches." Maples was separated from the rest of us, but that only made it easier to victimize him. During mealtimes, he had his own table, but we were the ones serving it. The other boys would spit in his food and put pubic hairs and dust balls in it. We would punch or slap him in the back of the head when we walked by as he was eating. Each day during showers, we were given a linen roll with an issue of towel, T-shirt, and briefs with our name taped across it. One of the linen boys decided to wipe his butt with a towel after defecating and rolled up Maples's linen with it. After that, it became amusing for everyone to use old linen to wipe themselves and reserve it for Maples's linen roll. Maples did not say anything else ever again, but it was too late for him.

At court, I was charged as an adult and transferred to the county jail. I was to be housed in the juvenile section until I turned eighteen. One day on the rec yard, I was watching a guy shooting hoops on the basketball court. Suddenly, I felt someone's arms cinch tightly around my neck. I looked down and saw a large spider web tattoo on the crook of the elbow. It was one of the Hispanic juveniles, nicknamed Spider. He was much bigger than me. I could not breathe and tried to pull down his arm, but he flexed even tighter and lifted me several inches off the ground. I blacked out and woke up on the ground, gasping for air, and saw stars everywhere. Spider and a group of Hispanics were laughing at me. They walked off as one of the deputies made his rounds.

One of the other Vietnamese kids saw me on the ground and helped me up. "Stay away from the Mexicans," he said. "If they try that again, we will have to fight all of them." I felt scared but knew I could not let him pick on me again because I could not be a victim. The juvenile section was filled with a bunch of kids who were all facing life sentences. Many of us still had not developed any sense of identity and distortedly thought that violence was the way to gain recognition. I wholeheartedly believed in it and felt ashamed that I had allowed Spider to choke me out.

A few weeks later, I was in a new dorm with two other Vietnamese and three Hispanics, including Spider. The Hispanics had been sniffing some drugs and were doing push-ups. They spoke in Spanish, and somewhere I realized their tones changed. I knew something was going to happen. One of them walked up to where we were playing cards and wanted to fight one of the Vietnamese. I looked down in hopes that nobody would call me out to fight, too. The cards trembled in my hands as they started fighting, and my heart was racing. But as the Vietnamese began to get the best of his assailant, it gave me courage. I saw Spider from the corner of my eye and walked up to him. "I wanna fight, Spider."

I knew after they were done, someone would want to fight me anyway—at least if I did it this way, I would be recognized for calling Spider out to fight first. Spider took one look at me, threw his head back, and began laughing. I took that opportunity and punched him square in the mouth. He reeled back, and I saw his lip was split. It threw him into a rage, and he threw me up against the bars of the cell and attacked me like a rabid dog. I protected myself as much as I could by covering up. He pounded on me, and the back of my head kept hitting against the bars as each of his blows hit my head and forearms.

Spider was roaring while swinging erratically, and he missed on one of the punches. I heard the sickening crunch of his hand breaking as it struck the bar. He screamed in pain, picked me up over his head, and body-slammed me onto the concrete floor. I landed on my lower back, and I heard a pop. The adrenaline was pumping through me, and even though I knew I was hurt, I pulled myself up on the bars. Spider's hands were a broken mess and he was gasping for air. Luckily, he did not attack me further.

The sound of keys jangling and boots stomping signaled that the deputies were coming. They cuffed all of us up for fighting. My back was throbbing, and they took us to the nurses to check for injuries. I said nothing about my intense back pain and denied I had been in a fight. I believed I could not say anything, or it would be considered snitching. The officers ended up separating us from the Hispanics, and for the next six weeks my dorm mates helped me get in and out of bed. Later, during my life sentence, I found out I had developed a degenerative disc from that injury.

On my eighteenth birthday, two deputies came down and started singing "Happy Birthday" to me. One of them sneered at me and said, "Are you ready to join the real men upstairs, juvie? Today is the day you get to go with the big boys."

I grabbed the few belongings I had: a book of stamps and some envelopes and paper to write letters. I fought back tears because the familiarity of my life these past several months had at least seemed a little comforting. Now I was going into somewhere new. I would be thrown into the mainline, where everyone who was arrested and fighting a court case was housed. I was unsure what to expect.

The mainline jail system was more organized with rules of how to conduct ourselves than juvenile hall. In each dorm of seventy men, there was one prisoner who was known as the House Mouse. The House Mouse was the intermediary between the prisoners and the deputies. Our House Mouse was a Samoan in his forties, with graying hair, known as Uso. He was heavyset and was always happy and smiling, although he was fighting a murder case. One day, Uso came back and called the heads of each race together. His bunk was next to mine, and I got to hear everything.

"OK, everyone, we got a fuckin' rapist in our dorm," Uso began. "I just saw the bed card from the deputy that is on right now. He says we have the green light to get him after shift change tonight.

He doesn't want to be here to do the paperwork when it goes down. We need a representative from each race to volunteer for the mission."

Each prisoner who came in had a bed card with their mug shot and arrest charges on it. In our pecking order, anyone who committed any type of sex offense is considered the lowest of the low. Gang murders are at the top of this spectrum, while everything else fell in between. Even deputies despised sex offenders, but I was still surprised to hear of one setting a rapist up.

I was new and felt out of place and only wanted to fit in with these guys. "I will volunteer and represent for the mission," I chimed in. I would end up regretting that decision.

Uso had a proud look on his face and looked at the heads of the whites, blacks, and Hispanics. "We got a representative for the Asians. If each of you get your representative, we will get this chester tonight after shift change." Chester was our slang for a sex offender.

After everyone walked off, Uso looked at me. "Listen, youngster, the cops will do body checks. Make sure you kick him instead of punching him." Body checks were where the deputies would look at our knuckles for red marks, scrapes, and swelling for evidence of a fight. Uso was giving me a tip to get away with the attack. I nodded and thanked him.

That night, at shift change, the cop on duty announced over the PA system that he was leaving and for us to have a good night. That was the signal for us to attack the rapist. The victim had already been pointed out to me, and my bunk was near where we were to attack him. The plan was for someone else to lure him to the dayroom, where people played cards and watched TV, and I saw him approaching. When he walked by my bunk area, I swung myself off and kicked him in the head. He dropped facedown, and four of us began to kick and stomp on him. He started screaming, but the more he screamed, the harder we kicked his head and body. He grew quiet. There was a pool of blood that began to come out from around his head, and he was not moving. One of the other attackers climbed up on a nearby bunk and jumped off, landing with both feet on the back of the victim's head. I heard a popping, squishing noise, and his head bounced off the concrete floor. We all stood in shocked silence. The attacker climbed up on the bunk and once again jumped with both feet onto the back of the man's head. This time, though, his feet slipped from all the blood everywhere, and he fell onto his butt. He had blood on his palms and the back of his jumpsuit from sitting in the blood. There was so much blood everywhere. I was breathing like I had run a thousand-yard sprint. I looked down at my shoes and pants and there were spots of blood on them.

I went into survival mode and began to wipe and clean my shoes. There were a lot more blood splatters on me than I had expected. The jail-issued shoes were the plastic gummy kind, and I was able to wipe off the blood quickly. I took off my clothes, threw them in a plastic bag, filled it up with soap and water, and tied the bag off. I let it sit in the corner of the dorm with other laundry that was being hand washed. I jumped in the shower and took a quick rinse. I was still breathing heavily, and my heart was still pounding. I looked down and noticed red welts on my legs from being accidentally kicked by the other men when we attacked the rapist. One of the other Vietnamese handed me some lotion and told me it would get rid of the red marks. I rubbed it in, and they began to fade.

Two of the other assailants were standing around, nonchalantly talking to the other men in the dorm and reliving the fight. I noticed they had changed their clothes, but I saw spots of blood still on their shoes. A lot of the people in the dorm had pitched in to help mop up the blood with towels, yet the victim still lay on the ground, unmoving. He began to groan from somewhere deep in his throat, and I could tell he was beginning to choke from lying facedown in his own blood.

Someone decided to roll him over onto his back. My bunk was nearby, and I had a clear view of what we had done to another human being. His whole body looked swollen, most of all his face, which had turned a deep purplish black. His eyes were bulging from their sockets, and he looked like a human fly. Blood and spittle were still bubbling up from the area where his nose and mouth used to be. I saw a purple crease that ran diagonally across his forehead, where his skull had caved in. The sight silenced the whole dorm.

The deputies were finally alerted that there was a man down. The first deputy who walked in took one look and ran back out, screaming into his walkie-talkie. Our dorm soon had what looked like the whole force of deputies inside, and true to protocol, they began to do body checks.

"Everyone, strip down!" one of the deputies screamed.

My heart was pounding in my chest as they came and looked at my knuckles with their flashlights, but they moved on. The two assailants who had not cleaned their shoes also had red welts on their legs. They were handcuffed and taken out, and word later came down that they were charged with attempted murder, since the victim was in critical condition. I had nightmares about what happened for months after that. Many times, I dreamed someone was stomping on my head until it burst open and feared sooner or later it would happen to me.

After that day, the older guys treated me differently. Before, it felt like they ignored me. But after the incident, I felt accepted and liked. They called me to their bunk areas and began indoctrinating me into the politics of prison life. They told me about how each race was separated into different groups, or cars. There were certain phones, toilets, sinks, and tables for each car to use. I learned each car was also responsible for the trash in their own backyard. This meant that if someone from a certain race messed up in some way, his car was responsible for cleaning up the mess. Cleaning up the mess usually meant beating up the guy in your own car, a member of your own race, for all the other races to see. I hoped nothing like that would ever happen to me.

Not long after, I had to clean up the trash in my backyard. The jail moved people around all the time, and I was moved to another dorm of seventy men. There was only one other Vietnamese there, named Coon. We went to the chow hall for breakfast and, upon returning, saw that someone had stolen some of our commissary food. The thief also took some of our brand-new jail-issued T-shirts. Brand-new T-shirts were valuable and hard to come by.

Coon had marked the collar of his T-shirts and spotted one of them being worn by a paisano, the group of Hispanics who did not speak much English.

"That fuckin' paisa over there has my shirt on." He pointed. "Let's fuck him up!" He began tightening up the laces on his shoes.

“Wait, we can’t do that,” I cautioned. I knew the thief would be beaten by his own people. “We have to let the paisas and their car know.”

Coon was a few years older and did not want to listen to some punk eighteen-year-old. “If you’re too scared, just stay right here and I will take care of this myself!” Of course I was scared, but I could not admit it. I tightened up the laces on my shoes and walked with him to confront the thief.

I thought Coon was going to start attacking the guy, and I was ready for that. Instead, he started screaming at the top of his lungs. “You fuckin’ thief! Give me back my shirts!”

He continued to curse at the guy and then grabbed at a T-shirt that was on the paisano’s bed. The paisano grabbed for the other end, hopped off, and they began a tug-of-war with it. The other paisanos began to surround us, and my mind screamed that we were in imminent danger. I was reminded about my nightmares of the man we stomped on and feared that was going to happen to us. There was no talking to the paisanos now; they were going to attack us. I saw only one way forward.

Coon and the thief were still in the tug-of-war. I squared up my hips and punched the thief in the face. He screamed in surprise, let go, and fell down. From the corner of my eye I saw Coon slip backward, off balance. It was a blur what happened next, as I was punched and kicked from everywhere. My only thought was to not fall down, and I tried to fight back as much as I could. There were so many of them everywhere, and I could no longer breathe.

Fists were still pounding me when the familiar jangling of keys caused everyone to stop. Deputies ran in the dorm and pulled Coon and me out. My eyebrow was split open, and I felt battered everywhere, but my head was still intact. That was all that mattered to me. Coon was in worse shape because they had stomped on him when he fell down. He had a golf ball-size lump on his left temple, and the whole side of his face was an angry red. We were both breathing heavy.

One of the deputies opened up a black folder. Inside were the bed cards and mug shots of everyone in the dorm. "Who attacked you, son?" he asked me in concern. I knew better than to cooperate.

"I don't know," I said.

"How about you?" he said, turning to Coon. "Can you point out who did this to you guys?" To my horror and disgust, Coon began pointing out several of our assailants.

We got rehoused in another dorm that same afternoon. There were several other Vietnamese, one of whom I already knew. I told him about the fight and how Coon snitched on our assailants. In the jail system, word travels fast. Once someone is known as a snitch, they are not safe anywhere. The last thing I wanted to be known as was as a snitch. I definitely could not be associated with one either.

Sure enough, the paisanos in our new dorm got word from our previous dorm that we had snitched. I saw a group of them come over and whisper to the older Vietnamese guys, and I saw people looking my way. I felt anxious. The Vietnamese had to clean up the trash in their car, and at this moment, I was considered trash. Coon told, not me, but I knew nobody would believe it unless I took care of it. I walked up to the older guys and volunteered to be one of the people who was going to beat up Coon. I was so afraid of being labeled a snitch and would do whatever was necessary to clear my name.

Coon knew what was coming when we attacked him and didn't put up a fight. He was so scared when we kicked and stomped him that he peed his pants. I had to get pulled off him because I kept kicking his head when he was already half-knocked out. I was frightened that anyone else might think I snitched, so I went above and beyond to show off and hurt him. I wanted to prove that I was not a snitch and believed the best way was to hurt another man excessively. A by-product of volunteering to inflict violence on others was the sense of acceptance and reputation I gained. The guys liked me and started referring to me as "Youngster." That's the nickname I carried into the gang life later.

My first large-scale race riot happened a little after that. A Vietnamese gang had a shootout on the streets, and stray bullets killed an innocent Hispanic boy coming out of church. It was all over the news. This caused a lot of tension, and the Mexican gangs put a green light on that Vietnamese gang. A green light meant all Mexican gang members were required to attack anyone from that gang. But many times, they would attack anyone that looked Asian. One of the Vietnamese in our dorm went out to court one day and ended up in the hospital because he was jumped by twenty Hispanics at court inside the holding tanks. I knew it was only a matter of time before I would get jumped. It was hard for me to sleep at night, and whenever people would group up and begin whispering, I broke out in a cold sweat. I kept imagining my head bursting open from being stomped on.

One evening, I heard my name called over the speakers to

report to the officer's sally port. They said to bring my bedroll and property, which meant I was getting housed in another dorm. This happened quite often, but because of the green light, I feared getting jumped in my new dorm. I stepped into the sally port and saw the most welcome sight. Sprawled all around inside the barred gates were about twenty other Vietnamese with their bedrolls. About half of them looked like they had recently been in fights, with black eyes and swollen lips.

The jail authorities decided to consolidate us into a designated collection of dorms. They finally realized that all Asians were getting jumped throughout the jail and thought putting us together in bigger numbers would prevent it from happening. They were wrong. They moved us into another seventy-man dorm, but the races were still mixed. There was a palpable tension and fear in the dorm as we shuffled in.

"As soon as the cops close the gate, get out your knives and stab them all!" one of the guys shouted in Vietnamese. It was time for revenge, and many of the guys had toothbrushes sharpened to be used as knives. Others began to shove soap bars into empty socks to swing as weapons. One of them broke off a metal shower nozzle and handed it to me.

"Here, Youngster, put this inside your sock."

I shoved in the heavy piece of steel and knotted the end like I witnessed the other guys do with their soap bars. It had a nice comforting weight. I had never swung a sock as a weapon before, but I did not let anyone know that. The other races began to group up, the whites and Hispanics on one end and us on the other. Then we began attacking each other. It was utter chaos, and I swung my weapon as hard as possible at anyone who I saw was not Vietnamese. I had been scared all these months and tired of being picked on. These faces represented all the groups who picked on me. Hispanics had picked on me. Whites had picked on me. I was in jail because some whites threatened to kill my family. They were all the reason why everything was wrong with my life at that moment, and they were going to pay for it. Every time I struck someone, there was a satisfying crunch.

I did not know it at the time, but that was where I began to hate and resent all other races and, eventually, become a racist. I finally felt accepted and knew where my place was in the world. I finally found where I belonged, and it was against every other race. I believed we were superior and looked down on anyone who was not my race.

Years later, this us-versus-them mentality would turn me against everyone else in the world, including my family. One of the angriest conversations with my mother was during my time incarcerated in the Youth Authority. I was fascinated with the writings of Karl Marx, George Jackson, Ho Chi Minh, and other revolutionaries. I loved that they spoke about fighting against an unjust system since I felt I was a victim of an unjust system.

During one of our visits, she suggested I should be praying.

I grew angry and yelled, "Why should we pray to a god that does not exist?"

There was so much anger inside me at the world, God, and where I was in life. I told my mom we should not be praying to a white god and that the concepts that she believed in were all fake. Tears welled in her eyes and she stood in silence as I continued stabbing her with my words. I let her know that our family had fought on the wrong side of the war and we were traitors to our race.

She muttered, "Your father would be saddened to hear what you are saying. Your grandfather was thrown in a concentration camp, and our family and many others lost our country because of the Viet Cong."

I looked at her and whispered, "I wish I had been born twenty years earlier. I would have been a freedom fighter, and a revolutionary, and would have fought to liberate our country with the Viet Cong."

My mom gasped.

"Please don't talk to me about any white god," I continued. "I don't want to hear any of that anymore." I was so certain that I finally knew who I was. Yet, if that were so, why was I still searching?

CHAPTER 5

FADE TO BLACK

PRESIDING COMMISSIONER: OK. And why'd you have a gun?

INMATE HUYNH: I had a gun because I was part of a very violent gang. I had a gun because I wanted to carry it. It gave me a sense of power. It gave me a sense of control of my life. It gave me a sense of feeling powerful and an image of "Hey, I'm somebody."

PRESIDING COMMISSIONER: And had you ever shot it before?

INMATE HUYNH: Yes. I was part of a very violent gang, Commissioner. I've shot the gun before.

PRESIDING COMMISSIONER: Had you shot it at other individuals, other people?

INMATE HUYNH: Yes, I have.

By the time I paroled from the California Youth Authority, I was quite lost, confused, and angry at the world. Coming home after spending a couple of years inside felt unfamiliar to me. I definitely did not see the world the same way anymore. I was a stranger in a world that had moved on. Everywhere I went, I was ashamed because I thought people could tell I just got out. I had lost contact with most of my friends from high school. When I ran into old friends, it was awkward to hold a conversation with them. I could tell they were hesitant to talk to me because they heard I had been locked up.

I did what I thought would be best: enroll in college and try to rebuild my life. It was difficult to find jobs because of my criminal conviction, so I did part-time work at different companies. The gang lifestyle, though, was prevalent in the Vietnamese community in the early '90s. Even though I was in college, it was normal to be part of a gang. The gang culture gave me a sense of completeness and acceptance, and my life revolved around being with my homeboys, whatever they were up to.

During one of my first weekends home, I was shot at for the first time. We were headed to a park to watch a fight between one of my friends and some guy he had a beef with. It was late in the evening, and we pulled up to the park and turned off the car lights. I was sitting in the back seat and lit up a cigarette. Most fights could escalate quickly, so two of the guys in my car had brought along guns for our protection. Just knowing we had a couple of guns made me nervous but at the same time reassured. I was on active parole and knew I had no business being there. But I did not say a word. These guys had heard of me from the inside, and I did not want to diminish my reputation in their eyes.

I remained quiet in the back of the car, smoking one cigarette after another. Soon enough, I saw headlights of several cars pulling up to the park. One of the cars stopped next to us. Four people sat inside, all wearing dark bandanas over their faces, with their windows rolled down. One of the guys in the back pulled out a shiny silver handgun and aimed at us. I ducked, my cigarette fell on the floor of the car, and the whole world erupted into gunfire all around. Square window fragments fell on my face. I felt the car move as it screeched off. Some more shots rang out, and I could not tell if we were shooting or being shot at. My ears were ringing, and the smell of gunpowder, a smell I became intimately familiar with later on, filled the car. I opened my eyes and saw my cigarette still lit on the floor. I smashed it out with my foot and kicked it under the seat in front of me so nobody could see it and sat back up. I touched myself all over to make sure I was OK. Our car had been hit a few times, and the front passenger window had shattered, but nobody in the car was hit.

It was strangely exhilarating and exciting, yet I never wanted that to happen to me again. Within a couple of weeks, I got my hands on a gun and carried it whenever we met up for trouble. Not until many years later did I see the irony in not wanting to be shot but still being OK with shooting people. Having a gun alleviated my fear of feeling helpless and added to my reputation on the streets.

Whenever I experienced things that scared me, I never wanted it to happen again. Therefore, I resolved to do it first. Getting choked out led me to attack people first. Watching another man get his head stomped out made me never put my head down or lie on the ground in a fight. Seeing someone get beaten up for snitching made me never consider snitching on anyone. Getting shot at without a gun caused me to get one and shoot at others first. That worked for me until the time I ran out of bullets.

It was my homegirl Smurfette's birthday. She was like the older sister I never had, and we always hung out together. We drank and had deep conversations about life and the world. She encouraged me to leave the gang and figure out something for my life, yet every weekend they were all we hung out with. She told me that I was meant for much more. At the time, it fell on deaf ears.

We were at a nightclub when rival gang members arrived. We recognized them from their gang attire: sandals, oversized slacks, and ball caps. We referred to them as fresh off the boat, or FOBs, because they could not speak English well. We threw punches at each other, knocked over some tables, and security kicked us out. I had guns inside my car, and we planned an ambush at a nearby commercial street. Since these enemies all knew my car, they would naturally follow us. Everyone else was supposed to head for the freeways, and we would meet up after the ambush.

There were two carloads of them following us slowly down the dark street. One of my homeboys, Sandman, jumped out and hid about a hundred yards behind us, along the path they would take. The plan was simple. Sandman was to let them drive past him toward my car, which was parked at the end of the street, and open fire when he had a good angle. We would turn my car around one of the buildings, come out from a parking lot right behind where they entered, and then join in the shooting. Then we could pick up Sandman and make our escape.

Of course, the plan fell apart. For some reason, Smurfette's car pulled up next to mine after we dropped off Sandman. Gunshots started ringing out, and I knew Sandman had started shooting. I heard different shots and knew they were shooting back at Sandman. We had to go help him!

"Smurfette! Get on the freeway. Do not follow my car!" I shouted. She nodded, and we sped off. To this day, I am not sure if she heard what I said or not. There were too many shots ringing out. We pulled the car around, and the sound of more gunshots rang through the streets. As we came around the building behind them, I thought for sure they were out of bullets. Our driver slowed down, and we opened fire on a couple of the idiots who had stepped out of their cars. They began shooting back an inordinate amount of shots. I could not comprehend how they could have so many bullets!

We turned down the street, and Sandman jumped in breathless. "Those fuckers are crazy, dude! One of them was running at me, shooting with his sandals on like he was still in Vietnam!" he exclaimed. Smurfette's car was right in front of us, headed for what looked like a nearby freeway.

Our conversation was cut short as the sound of a car coming up behind us had us all turn around. I aimed at the driver and began shooting in hopes of slowing them down. Bang, bang, bang! Three quick shots and the slide on my gun locked back, exposing the barrel. I was out of bullets.

"I'm out of bullets! Don't let them pull up next to us!" I yelled.

"Fuck! I am out too," muttered Sandman. Our driver floored the gas pedal, but the other car continued to gain ground on us, and they were still shooting. We came to an intersection, braked hard, screeched, swerved, and made a hard left turn. My body shifted to the right, and I saw the green traffic lights swirl around me. The pursuing vehicle didn't have time to react but instead continued to chase Smurfette's car.

I do not know if they were shooting at her car or not, but she tried to make a hard right turn at an intersection and instead hit the light pole. She was thrown from the car but was still alive according to the first witness at the scene. Smurfette bled to death on the cold black asphalt that night.

Smurfette's death was humiliating to our gang. Someone had killed one of ours, and until we retaliated, we had lost face on the streets. We all knew what we had to do, yet I saw the hesitancy in some of my homeboys. Instead of acknowledging the fear in myself, I became disgusted at many of them. I never wanted anything like this to happen again, so I bought some high-capacity clips. I thought more bullets would be the answer to it all.

Of all places, Smurfette was buried at the same cemetery as my father. Her death put me in a dark place. She loved alcohol; I would buy some, go to her grave in the evenings, and inebriate myself while pouring some on the ground for her as a sign of respect. Many times, I did not even visit my father's grave while there. After I was drunk, I would go hunting for the group who was responsible for her death. Even if I did not find them, I always found other gang members to shoot at.

By the summer of 1995, at age twenty-one, I lost any perspective of what it meant to have a soul and no longer saw other gang members as even half humans but as targets to take my anger out on.

There were numerous shootings over the next few years, but one in particular stands out. One night, I was passed-out drunk in the back seat of my Acura Integra as my brother drove us home. While at a stoplight, a car pulled up next to our passenger side and opened fire. I woke up disoriented, my ears ringing, and saw my brother slouched over the center console armrest. The buckle to the automatic seat belts where his head had been was shattered. Square window shards were all over his shoulders and in his hair. I felt sick to my stomach. Cold air was streaming in through the passenger window.

My brother finally moved and miraculously was not hit anywhere. He said it was a black Honda Accord that had opened fire on us. When he described the rims that it had, I knew which particular gang had tried to kill us. These guys knew my car, and I was furious that they had ambushed us like that. My brother had almost died because of my gang ties. The next opportunity I had, I was going to kill any and all of them, I told myself.

The next day, we drove to Los Angeles. My friend had an auto body shop that would fix the damage to my car. While they were working on it, I kept thinking about my brother and what had happened. Part of me wished this could all stop, but the only way I saw it ending was with more violence. I could not wait to find these fuckers slipping on the streets. They were all going to pay.

The repairs took all day, and it was dark when we almost got home. At a traffic light, I noticed movement in a black Honda Accord several cars behind us. There were four guys inside pulling on ski masks. It was the attackers from the night before! Instinctively, I wanted to jump out and open fire, but there were too many witnesses around. I knew they would follow us and instructed my brother to turn down a series of residential streets, then jumped out with my gun and an extra clip.

"Keep the headlights on, and turn the car and block the street,"

I ordered him. He hesitated. "Just do it!" I yelled. I ran back up the way the Honda Accord would be coming and hid between two parked cars on the side in which the driver of their vehicle would be closest to me.

I already played out in my mind how this would go down. My enemies would drive up and see the taillights of my car stopped ahead. They would slow down or stop while they figured out what to do. That is when I would come from their blind side and take two shots at their car. Their natural instincts would be to duck down. From there, it would be like shooting fish in a barrel. I would run up and unload at the driver first, so he could not move the car. The other three would still be ducking, and it would be a matter of emptying my first clip at the rest of them. Then I would reload the second clip and make sure they were all dead. *How dare they try to kill me and my brother*, I thought. *Didn't they know who I was? Didn't they know who they were messing with?*

Inside my car was the last clip; this would be for the getaway in case police responded. I knew committing multiple murders would get me the death penalty, and I was not going to get caught.

The sound of a car horn and my brother yelling at me shook me out of my murderous thoughts. It was hard to understand what he was saying, but he had my attention. He must have spotted a police car or something. I ran back to my car and jumped in. We took off, and my brother looked at me.

"You were going to kill those guys back there! What are you doing? What is wrong with you?" He looked at me like he did not know me. I couldn't believe my brother had called me back to the car because he did not want me to kill these guys!

"Fuck that," I justified. "They were trying to kill us last night, and they were going to try again tonight. I could have wiped them all out tonight, and their gang wouldn't be about shit no more."

We did not speak about it further, but something had shifted between my brother and me. It bothered me the way my brother had looked at me. That was the night I knew I was alone in the world because nobody understood how I now saw it.

CHAPTER 6

STUDYING THE ENEMY

PRESIDING COMMISSIONER: So how long did you spend in CYA?

INMATE HUYNH: They gave me a seven-year CYA term for conspiracy to commit a crime. I did about two-and-a-half years total, I think. Around there. I got out in the end of 1993.

PRESIDING COMMISSIONER: For the record, you were arrested on March 16,1992for Attempted Murder, convicted of Conspiracy to Commit a Crime out of Orange County, committed to CYA. On February 16th,1996you were convicted of Felon in Possession of Firearm. What kind of sentence did you get for violating parole?

INMATE HUYNH: They gave me a two-year violation, and I got out in 1998.

PRESIDING COMMISSIONER: OK. The date of this commitment offense was January 15th,1999You were convicted by jury November 3rd, 2000. And then you were received at CDCR on December 26th, 2000.

INMATE HUYNH: Yes.

In 2007, a landmark ruling came down from the California Supreme Court regarding life-term prisoners, referred to as *In re Lawrence*. I was at Soledad State Prison and in the eighth year of my life sentence. I got my first glimmer of hope, but it did not last long.

Sandra Lawrence was a woman who was in for the murder of her lover's wife, a heat-of-passion killing that she committed in 1971. She was a fugitive for twelve years and eventually turned herself in. She was sentenced to seven years to life and was eligible for parole in 1990. From 1993 to 2005, she was granted parole four times, but all three governors reversed her parole grants. They all cited what became a catch-all term, "severity of the crime," and "public safety." It was a politicized process, and no governor would ever want to be soft on crime. Actual numbers are unclear, but from 1977 to 2007 less than 1 percent of all lifers ever got to go home, probably closer to 0.01 percent. From 1999 to 2003 of all the parole hearings conducted, there were only 371 parole grants. Of those, only nine were upheld and released. There were over 20,000 lifers at the time, and many of them had gone several times to the parole board during that window. Most of those releases were ex-police officers and other people who were well connected in some way. The lifer population believed that parole grants were a sham of the board. Each board commissioner was appointed by the governor. They granted only a small number, all of which were overturned by the governor.

In re Lawrence stated that the use of "severity of the crime" and citing "public safety" was not enough to overturn a parole grant. The inmate still had to show some signs of "current dangerousness." Still a vague term, but it was a small crack in the impossibly high walls of obtaining freedom. Even with the rulings, she was not released from prison by the board or governor. She wasn't freed until the courts stepped in and ordered her released.

The lifer population began to share the information of how she was able to win her freedom. Men inside the prison's law library began to make copies of the case law and share it. Inside every law library were a group of inmates we referred to as the Legal Beagles. These were the jailhouse lawyers, guys who filed writs and other legal work in the courts for other prisoners. Some of these guys knew case law inside out, while others only thought they did. After *In re Lawrence* was published, there were heated discussions between the Legal Beagles as they all had different interpretations of the court decision.

One day, I was standing at the concrete tables that belonged to our car, reading my copy of *In re Lawrence* that I obtained from one of the Legal Beagles. Each car had their own separate areas with tables and pull-up bars. One of the other lifers, Loose Tooth, was doing push-ups nearby. He was missing more than half of his teeth, and No Tooth actually would have been a better name for him. He had been down over twenty-eight years on a seven-year-to-life sentence. He had been denied so many times that he had given up hope and was quite resentful and bitter. He would particularly become agitated when anyone around him shared some good news. This day was no different.

"Hey, what are you reading?" he asked me in Vietnamese. Loose Tooth could barely speak English, and he could not read it at all.

"There's some case that came down, and they have to start giving lifers dates," I explained.

He looked at me like I was crazy. "Lifers dates? You believe that stuff? I have never seen a lifer get a date." He shook his head and walked away from me in disgust.

Many of the Legal Beagles were interesting in and of themselves. Like Loose Tooth, they had been denied many times by the board. They focused all their energy into fighting their cases in the courts. They studied case law and could cite how the courts and board and everyone else is breaking the law. They seemed particularly fascinated by people in positions of authority and would point out what they were doing wrong. Many times, these men came across as angry. Sometimes I would go in the law library and pick their minds, but I noticed many of the Legal Beagles themselves did not interpret the case law the same way. There were some that I would talk to, and they would state how certain cases would apply to us. But in reading over the same case, I realized I did not interpret it that way. I questioned my own comprehension because these were guys who had filed writs in the courts and other impressive things that I had never done.

When I met Al in the law library, I realized my understanding wasn't completely off. Al was in his fifties, with graying white hair and a thin mustache. He was always immaculately groomed in our prison-issued blues. His clothes were always ironed and tucked in, and he always seemed to walk with purpose. I noticed he rarely engaged in the discussions with the Legal Beagles, and when he spoke with people, it was with a reserved and quiet voice. One day, he noticed me in the law library.

"What are you reading there, young man?" he asked kindly. I was a bookworm; my way of escaping the monotony of prison life was to read. I had four books I checked out and, at any given time, had a habit of reading several books simultaneously. I showed him the books. He looked them over and slid them back to me. We began making small talk. We discussed what was going to be for dinner that evening even though nothing was ever great about dinner. He asked me what authors I enjoyed reading, how long I had been incarcerated, and if I was a lifer. Eventually, the conversation steered toward the Lawrence case, and I asked his interpretation of the ruling.

He explained to me that Lawrence was a favorable ruling for the lifer population but not to expect an immediate release for anyone. We would still have to go to the board, and the current political climate would not allow for anyone to get paroled. The only small chance for freedom was proving that the parole board did something wrong at the hearing that went against the Lawrence case. From there, we would have to file a writ like Sandra Lawrence had done, then try to get out through the courts. Of course, none of that would apply to me for at least another six years, when I would first be eligible for parole. I tucked his words into a corner of my mind for later reference.

Al was such a huge wealth of information. He was working in the finance industry before he got locked up. He had a business partner who had stolen his life savings from him. He ended up shooting him and was given a life sentence. I loved listening to him share his thoughts on politics, how he had created his businesses, and how he had traveled all over the world. Al began recommending other books for me to read, and then we would have deep discussions on various topics in those books.

Early on in my prison sentence at Pelican Bay, I did not associate with others outside our car. I looked down on anyone not of Asian descent and viewed my Vietnamese ethnicity as superior. After Pelican Bay, I transferred to Donovan State Prison. It was located near San Diego, known as a great prison to do time at because of the weather and the amount of programs it had. Donovan had sports leagues for basketball, volleyball, and softball. Little did I know I would be instrumental in creating another sports league through the use of some toilet paper, masking tape, and an old sock.

One Sunday, my friend Frank and I were watching football in the loud dayroom; we played in a fantasy league together and were rooting for the players on our squad. Frank was holding a roll of the prison-issued toilet paper that the building officer had given him. Each cell was issued two rolls of toilet paper a week, but a prisoner could request more from the officer when he ran out. On a whim, he looked at me, took a three-step drop like a quarterback, and said, "Catch this, homie!" and threw the roll of toilet paper. It spiraled through the air like a football at me, and I caught it. I threw it back, and after several more throws back and forth, the toilet paper loosened and began to flutter through the air, no longer spiraling like a football. I saw the boyish grin on Frank's face as we decided to wrap it with masking tape and then clothed it with an old sock. That evening, we brought our converted football to the yard and threw it around. Within several days, we had a pickup game with another race, and other groups built their teams to play against us. A few weeks later, Frank and I submitted a proposal for a football league to the prison officials. It was granted, we were issued real footballs on the yard, and Donovan now had its first-ever football league.

I grew up loving football, and the opportunity to be able to play it again gave me something exciting to look forward to each day. Football changed the dynamics of prison for me. I found exercise was a great way to clear my mind, and every time our yard opened, I was on the yard working out. Now with a football to throw around, I ran routes on the field for anyone who would throw me the ball. Although our football teams were divided by race, the competitive interaction actually contributed to easing a lot of the tension among each of the cars. There were many beliefs I had incorporated in my life up to that point, but my time at Donovan caused me to question them.

While interacting with other lifers, I found commonality in our shared struggle. Of course I never verbalized it because I was afraid people in my own car would think I was weak or soft. Because we were in prison, there were still racial politics that kept us in our place. My stay at Donovan lasted four years, then I transferred to Soledad prison.

Soledad was also cell living, but we did not have as many programs as Donovan. The politics at Soledad were more rigid, and we did not associate much with men from other races. Besides being involved in sports leagues, there were places on the prison yard that were considered "neutral." The law library was one of those places. Another place was the track, a concrete pathway that circled around the prison yard, tables, and workout areas. For some reason, most prisoners walked or jogged the track counterclockwise. It was like this at every prison I lived at.

Al would love to get in at least a few miles walking a day on the track. Since it was neutral territory, we would walk together and talk. Of course, the guys in my car began teasing me.

"Hey, Quan, why are you hanging out with that old white man all the time? Is he giving you candy, little boy?" Of course, many of the jokes were lighthearted, but I knew from experience that prison jokes can become a perception if not nipped in the bud. At that time, I only wanted to fit in and not be the one to cause any type of conflict for me or my race. Everything in there, for me, was about image and reputation. So I kept my interactions with Al to the bare minimum: occasional conversations at the law library or track. I definitely did not want to be put in a position to have to fight with someone to prove myself.

Lots of times in prison, I saw people get into arguments over the most trivial things. One of the most ridiculous fights I saw started because of a hot link. One evening, we were in the chow hall, and four of us were sitting at one of the steel tables. One of the older guys sitting at our table was Mr. Park. He was one of those guys who incessantly talked and bragged about himself. He was intelligent, but his lack of awareness, in combination with his oversized ego, made him unbearable to be around. I tried to avoid him as much as possible. We sat down for dinner, and he was already talking about how much revenue his business on the outside had generated in the past week. Sitting next to him was Tung, a quiet guy who had transferred in from another prison.

I politely nodded my head while Mr. Park continued to talk. He then picked up his hot dog bun with a hot link inside and took a big bite into it. The other end of the casing burst, and the juices squirted all over Tung's hair and face.

Without missing a beat, Mr. Park proclaimed, "Damn, my bad. Looks like I busted a nut all over his face." Tung reached for a napkin, wiped his face, then looked at Mr. Park and punched him. The fight did not last too long before the correctional officers broke them apart and took them to the hole.

Many times, men fought because of what we deemed as disrespect. If someone bumped into a person and did not apologize, it was considered disrespect. Questioning someone's masculinity was disrespect. Calling someone a bitch, punk, or snitch was the worst form of disrespect. The bursting of the hot link on Tung's face, coupled with Mr. Park's sexual comment, was disrespectful, and we all agreed that Tung had no choice but to attack Mr. Park. Many years later, I realized this term we referred to as "disrespect" was an umbrella that we hid all our feelings under. Tung could simply say Mr. Park disrespected him and have all rights to fight Mr. Park. In prison, that is all that was needed. The real underlying feeling, though, was closer to humiliation, and even fear, that someone would view Tung as weak. I know that because many times I hid my fears and feelings underneath that same catch-all word, *disrespect.*

To make sure I was not disrespected, I did not associate with Al as much as I would have liked. I noticed throughout my journey, though, that at every prison, there were several Als. On a yard with several thousand other men, there were always men to talk to and learn from. My thirst for knowledge and wisdom began with learning from those who experienced so much in their lifetimes. There is a lot of untapped collective wisdom from them.

After *In re Lawrence* was published, I transferred to Solano State Prison. There, I discovered something much more valuable than learning from other men. In the California prison system, after a lifer goes to a board hearing, they are issued a transcript. Each hearing was transcribed, and the exact words of the prisoner and the commissioners were in it. Some of the men stored it with their legal paperwork and never looked at it again. Some threw it away. A very rare few used their transcripts to petition the courts for relief, as Sandra Lawrence had done. Yet, nobody shared their transcripts with each other because it had all the ugly, dark, dirty secrets from each person's case transcribed in there. Plus, we all believed nobody was ever going home anyway.

At Solano, we were housed in buildings that each had twenty-four dorms, with anywhere from ten to sixteen men packed up in each dorm. The dorms had low partition walls to separate them, but there was no cell door to keep a prisoner locked in. The dorms were about twice the size of the cells I was used to, but we now had at least five times the amount of people in it. Up until this time, I had only lived in cell living, so Solano was an adjustment for me. The dorms were packed, yet I liked how we were no longer locked in a cell and able to walk in and out at will. Most of the prisoners congregated in the dayroom to play cards, dominoes, or talk.

One of my first friends at Solano outside my race was an old African American man named Alabama. Over the years, I developed an affinity for older prisoners. They had so much untapped wisdom to share. Alabama was called 'Bama for short. He always seemed to have a thin discharge of mucus in his eyes that he never wiped away. He liked to sit in the dayroom with a denim jacket and beanie on, even in the middle of the hot summer. Every once in a while, I sat down with him and we would play a couple of card games of rummy. He moved slow and was not good at the game, but I enjoyed his company and conversation. He had been in over thirty years on a seven-to-life sentence. He told me how he had gone to the board so many times that he forgot, close to a dozen. He quit showing up to his scheduled hearings years ago. One afternoon, he was sitting at one of the dayroom tables sorting through a pile of legal work. He was up for transfer and couldn't take everything with him.

There was a pile of maroon folders on the table, and I knew

those to be the hearing transcripts. I had never read one before. He opened up the bindings and tore up the individual pages.

"'Bama, what are you throwing away your transcripts for? Don't you need them to file paperwork in the courts?"

"I ain't ever going home. These will take up room in my box. My court appeals got shot down years ago. I don't need them anymore. Plus, I stopped showin' up to them hearings years ago." He always forgot about things he already told me.

Alabama began to tell me the same thing he had told me in dozens of our conversations, that the board twists your words and looks for reasons to deny you parole, and it was all a sham. He stated again that he had quit going years ago. I let him continue to talk as he opened up the butterfly bindings on each transcript and tore up the pages, one by one. He had a commercial trash can next to our table and was throwing the transcripts in it. I liked hearing from people what happened at the board because I had no clue what to expect.

Something told me those transcripts were going to show me exactly what happened. I did not know how to ask for them from 'Bama. I began to work up the courage several times but each time found an excuse or distraction to not say anything. He was down to the last few transcripts. He began flipping through them, and for some reason, he looked up at me. "Here, you can have a look at this one. It was the last time I went to the board in '02."

It had been seven years since he had even showed up to a hearing.

I read through the transcript and it opened my eyes; it showed everyone's words as they said them on the record. While reading it, I realized what Alabama had told me happened, and what actually transpired in the hearing were two different things. In the beginning, Alabama's hearing was mostly procedural. The commissioners read into the record his case history, county of conviction, background information, and facts of the case. Then the commissioners got right into it and asked Alabama his crime. As I read, I noticed the person who was answering seemed only a shell of the man I knew to be Alabama. The hearing seemed adversarial, and it made me feel quite intimidated. They were twisting his words from previous hearings and constantly seemed to insinuate that he was being dishonest. Alabama was stuttering, could not answer many questions, and was at times being evasive in his answers. Of course, I did not say anything to him about it but continued to skim through and read as much as I could of the hearing. My stomach felt sick, and I was already thinking of how my own hearing was going to go and what was going to be said to me. I finished and slid the transcripts back to Alabama.

He looked at me with his rheumy eyes and said, "Now you see why I don't go no more." Alabama transferred to a different prison, and I never saw him again. The transcripts opened my eyes to how the board process was conducted. It gave me a great chance to understand the enemy, and contrary to what most prisoners believed, the enemy was not the board commissioners but ourselves. We did ourselves the most harm by the things we said and did not say. I saw that now but had no clue how to solve that dilemma and overcome my own worst adversary.

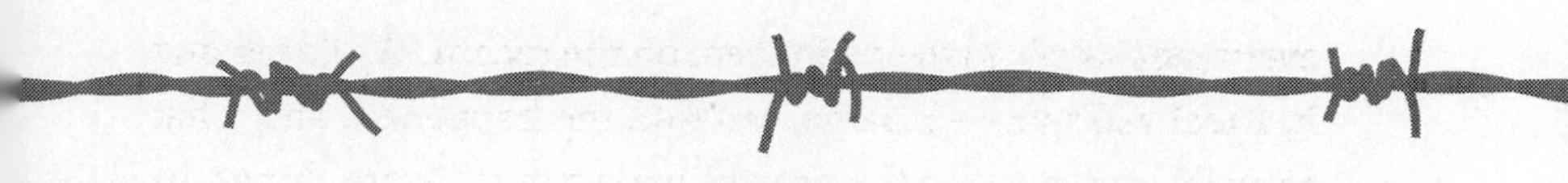

CHAPTER 7

BOOKS OF THE SAINTS

PRESIDING COMMISSIONER: When did you get involved in street gangs?

INMATE HUYNH: When I went into the California Youth Authority, juvenile hall and to county jail.

PRESIDING COMMISSIONER: Why did you join a street gang?

INMATE HUYNH: I joined a street gang at that time because it gave me a sense of acceptance and belonging with my Vietnamese peers.

PRESIDING COMMISSIONER: What do you think of gangs today, sir?

INMATE HUYNH: I think they are a cancer on society. I think a gang's only purpose is to just take from the community and destroy things that are in the community. They do nothing for the community.

During that time, I was heavily involved with all the criminal enterprises on the yard. I had my hand in the gambling rackets, drug and tobacco trade, and the smuggling of cell phones. Solano's politics were not as rigid as other prisons I had been at, and although there were still racial lines, the tension was nonexistent, and it was all about making money. Asians were considered neutral in prison politics, which gave us a competitive advantage in the hustling game. We could be intermediaries or brokers for most transactions on the yard, whereas the other races could not directly deal with each other. Because of that, I knew all the major players in the underground economy of prison and was connected to an extensive network.

Most of these players had gang ties. This network supported my belief that gang members were at the top of the hierarchy and fueled the shallow part of me that chased recognition. Together, we plotted how to bring contraband into the prison. I told myself I was providing a service for the other prisoners and never once thought about how I was preying on them and their family members on the streets, since it was family who usually paid for these transactions.

This went on for several years. It was like a game of cat and mouse with the prison officials; they knew I was up to something but not sure what. I finally got busted with some cell phones and tobacco in quick succession, and the prison deemed me a program failure. A program failure meant a prisoner could not follow the rules on the mainline and would be sent to solitary confinement. I was sentenced to 270 days in the hole. Since none of my charges were violent, though, they kept me on the yard and took away all my privileges: no recreational yard, no television or CD player, no visits, no phone calls. I was limited to my dorm twenty-three hours a day, allowed just one hour to get some exercise and shower.

Between sleeping and reading, I leaned on the low wall that

divided our dorms from each other and watched the routines of the men in the building. In one corner, a group of blacks would be working out at the same time every day. Once they finished, a group of Hispanics would use that time to do their exercise routine. At the dayroom tables, the same group of guys sat at the same tables every day, playing chess, pinochle, or dominoes. I became a silent observer and noticed many different characters.

For example, there was Success, an African American who sat at the same table day in and day out and played chess. He wore the same clothes each day: one gray sweatshirt worn as pajama pants, his legs coming out through the sleeves, and a prison-issued blue chambray shirt, the top three buttons fastened. The blue shirt would always part around his white T-shirt, showing his potbelly underneath. On his head was a beanie made out of another sweatshirt sleeve. He referred to himself in the third person. Every time he won his chess game, he would do a grotesque little dance and mock, "Told you, Success gonna get that ass!" Success had been down over thirty-two years, and as he said it, "Success ain't ever goin' home."

Then there was Fred, who had been in for over twenty years. Everyone knew he killed his stepfather because he would be the first to share it. He claimed that his stepfather had been molesting his sister and abusing his mother. Freddie would always have a constant scowl on his face and wore headphones around his neck. When he became upset, his whole face would become beet red. Lots of guys would go out of their way to get Freddie upset just for the reaction. For some reason, Freddie liked to come down to the low partition wall by my bunk and talk to me. He had this habit, though, as many men do in prison, of not making eye contact when talking with someone. He would lean up one side of the wall with his back to me, and I would be on the other side of it, propped up by my elbows, both of us looking out over the dayroom. Freddie would constantly complain to me about the other men who were in our building.

Todd was one of those guys who could help you get whatever you needed. He would help people get signed up for an upcoming church event and in the same day sell some heroin that he was moving for someone else. To have him tell it, "I'm just tryin' to help people find what they lookin' for." He knew I liked fresh vegetables, and he had a connection to the prison kitchen. At least a couple of times a week, he would stop by my bunk area and sell me an assortment of onions, bell peppers, or a head of cabbage. Todd was in for a kidnap robbery. He told me that had he known the board would keep him over twenty-eight years on a seven-to-life sentence, he would have been better off killing someone.

One day, I noticed Todd sat at a table with his parole hearing transcripts in front of him. He sat across from one of the Real Talk guys. They were a group of old-time lifers, most of them African American, most of them in for over thirty years. For some reason, though, these guys still had not lost hope and had created public speaking events called Real Talk. I remember attending a couple of these talks and admiring their courage to be able to get up and speak. They spoke about the board, the recent court rulings, and how we could actually start going home.

I had been hearing about the *In re Lawrence* case for several years and over that time saw only a handful of men that got released. Most of them were in their sixties, had done upward of thirty years, and had exemplary prison records. But I started seeing guys from Real Talk go to the parole board and get found suitable. Of course, the governor always reversed the findings, and they still had to fight their cases to the courts, similar to *In re Lawrence*. These Real Talk guys had a certain confidence and joy in their demeanor. Everyone knew them as the guys to talk to if you wanted to find out anything about the board. They were all willing to help people as long as they were on the straight and narrow, unlike me.

As I watched Todd, I noticed he looked uncomfortable. Freddie was leaned up against the wall next to me.

"That's Donnie over there sitting with Todd. He works up in the lens lab. He is one of those Real Talk guys that thinks they can help people go home." Freddie snickered. "Those guys really think they are somebody. I remember him from Folsom. You can't forget that big head of his anywhere." He adjusted his headphones around his neck and then continued to talk incessantly about everyone else in the dayroom. I had tuned Freddie out.

A little while later, Todd came by my bunk area with a fresh onion.

"Hey, Todd, what were you and that Real Talk guy doing at the table earlier?" I asked.

"Oh, he helpin' me get ready for the board. He gonna come each week to sit down wit' me. They finally lettin' lifers go home, and I'm gonna go, too. I done way too much time already." He paused. "Sheeit. There ain't no reason I should still be in prison after twenty-eight years. I didn't kill no one."

I did, though, I thought to myself.

I began to peel the onion so that I could add it to my Top Ramen noodles. "So do these Real Talk guys only help black folks?" I joked with Todd. "They won't help no Asian folks go home, would they?"

"Quan, ain't no way you goin' home. Look at you. You just got busted. You ain't done twenty-five years yet. You can't even leave your bunk area. What make you think you can leave prison?" We both laughed at the hilarity of it all.

Success jumped in on the conversation. "When Success go home, that when you got action. Success ain't goin' home, you ain't goin' home. You only been in eleven years. You better stop thinkin' that and just do your time, Youngster!" He adjusted the sweatshirt around his legs and shuffled back out to the dayroom for another game of chess.

That night, I lay in my bed and thought it all over. I would not go to the parole board for another three years, and I still did not know what I was going to do. There were a handful of guys on the yard, mostly from the Real Talk group, who had been found suitable by the board. They were waiting for the governor to review their cases, which took around 150 days. There was a mandated 120 days for review, plus an additional 30 days for approval from the governor. Of course, finally hearing about guys who were found suitable gave me hope that perhaps one day I, too, might get to go home. There was another part of my mind that I had not touched on yet, though, where all my darkest secrets were. That dark abyss told me I was going to die in prison.

The following week, I was lying in my bunk reading *A Game of Thrones* when the building officer called my name over the PA system and told me to report to their desk. *This was not good*, I thought to myself. I walked out of my dorm toward the podium, and Donnie from Real Talk was standing there with the officer. They both watched me as I approached.

The officer said to me, "Donnie is here to give you an intervention." He looked at Donnie, shook his head, and said, "Good luck with this one." He crossed his arms back over his potbelly and began to scan the dayroom. "Let me see how I can fight crime today. I know these guys are up to something." He got up and began walking, his keys jingling as he walked throughout the building, announcing his presence to everyone that he was on the move.

Donnie and I both looked at each other and laughed. He directed me to one of the tables in the dayroom. He sat down at one of the four seats, and I sat to his right. Donnie shook his head and pointed at the seat across from him. I slid to the seat and put my hands on the cold, metal table. He stared at me and said, "So Todd tells me you think I only want to help black folks go home." It was not a question.

I laughed hesitantly. "You can help people go home? How?"

"Well, I am not here to help you go home. I am here to see who you are, get a feel for your self-understanding, and see how we can get you on the path to demonstrate that you are no longer a danger to society." His emphasis had me curious.

"How do I…demonstrate it?" I asked.

Donnie looked at me and said, "Tell me about yourself."

I did not know how to answer, so began fumbling through my

words. "Well, I've been down for eleven years, in for second-degree murder. It was gang related." I always had to make sure everyone knew my case was gang related. Definitely did not want anyone to think I had killed a girlfriend or loved one. I rambled on, "They put me on C-status for 270 days because of cell phones and tobacco. I started my time at Pelican Bay and then from there transferred to—"

"Hold up." He held up his hands, and I noticed they were rather large, almost like catcher's mitts. "I had asked you to tell me about yourself. I did not ask you to tell me how long you have been in, for what, or even why you are on C-status." He breathed in, then said, "Tell me about yourself, Quan."

I looked down at the metal table and noticed the old graffiti marks that men had scratched into the table over the years. My eyes scanned the dayroom. I wanted to look everywhere but at Donnie. *Is this why Freddie never looks at anyone in the eyes?* I had not felt so self-conscious in years and was at a loss for words.

Donnie then started, "My name is Donnie. I grew up in…" As he continued talking, I found myself in awe of how he described himself. I do not remember the exact words, but I got the image of a man who was OK with all his faults and his failures and how he had overcome them all. He was content and happy and was not giving up, despite doing over twenty-five years on a seven-to-life sentence. He finished and looked at me. There was a knowing look of amusement on his face. "Don't worry, Quan. We'll get you there one day." He slid over a piece of paper and drew a line across the bottom. "OK, let's say this is your life timeline. I want you to label out significant events in your life."

I looked down at the line and drew one vertical hash. "This is where my father died." I drew several more. "Here is my first arrest. Here is where I was found guilty at trial and given my life sentence. This is where I was sent to Pelican Bay. This is when I went to Donovan. Here is where I was transferred to Soledad. And now, I am here at Solano."

"Quan, I notice that you only described the bad events that happened to you. Tell me, what do you like about yourself?"

Like about myself? I thought. I was scrambling to figure out how to answer; I was not sure what I liked about myself. Donnie continued to look at me. I was uncomfortable, so I lashed back out at him. "What is the point of all this anyway? How does any of this help me at the board? I got a life sentence because I was snitched on by my homeboy. Those dudes had it coming anyway. I am here on C-status because some snitches in here told on me!" After the words left my mouth, I knew they sounded off, but I was not sure why.

"Quan, I had asked you what you liked about yourself, and you went off justifying to me why you are in prison for murder. You do realize the board would have bashed you over the head talking like that, right? You would be in the same boat as all these other lifers on this yard—never going home." He slid a book over to me. *Homecoming: Reclaiming and Championing Your Inner Child* by John Bradshaw. "Start reading this, and I will be back next week." He sighed. "We have quite a bit of work to do."

I was quite discouraged after my talk with Donnie. I was horrified that I had been unable to name anything I liked about myself. I went and lay down in my bed and opened up the book he had given me. In it, I learned about what the author called the wounded inner child, also known as the unresolved issues from childhood and adolescence. These still very much affected me. I learned that this wounded inner child needed to be reclaimed and that I needed to champion him if I was to continue growing as a responsible, balanced, and healthy adult. These were terms that I was unfamiliar with, yet suddenly I had a glimmer of hope in my life. Until I opened the book, I didn't realize how much self-loathing and self-hatred I had developed over the years.

Donnie continued to come every week, and I began to ravenously read at least two books a week that drew my attention. I found books that were recommended from other prisoners or in discarded piles in the dayroom. Books with titles such as *Self-Esteem*, *Change Your Thinking Change Your Life*, *The Prophet*, *Road Less Traveled*, and *Emotional Intelligence*. Hidden treasures that were there for me to read all these years and I never saw them! I was excited to try and draw lessons from each book and apply them to my life.

My first bunky at Pelican Bay had given me a blue spiral-bound notebook that I never used, yet held on to throughout the years. Some of the pages were tattered and coming loose around the spine, but I now had a use for it. I jotted down quotes that resonated with me, and my blue notebook was soon filled up with scrawls and notes about particular areas of my life I wanted to refine, influenced from each of the books I read. Many evenings while restricted to my dorm, I read at the low wall, and scribbled quotes in my blue notebook.

These spiritual giants helped transform the way I thought and how I saw the world. Many books felt like they were written to help me through my own struggle with darkness, and I noticed there was a recurring theme of not dealing with failure in my life. When my father died and I believed I was somehow responsible, I became resentful, rejected God, and never properly processed his death. When I failed my SATs in high school, I tried to escape by signing up for the reserves. When Gallup did not promote me, it was easier to find someone to take it out on instead of facing why I was not a fit.

In my dorm, I examined why I felt so averse to anything that might cast me in a bad light and how that influenced me to lie to myself and make my choices. I found many quotes that resonated with me, shedding light on how I began my journey into darkness:

"Failure wounds our pride, and it is the wounded animal who is vicious. In the healthy organism failure will be a stimulus to self-examination. But since the evil individual cannot tolerate self-criticism, it is in time of failure that he or she will inevitably lash out one way or another."

—M. SCOTT PECK, *THE PEOPLE OF THE LIE*

"The longer we continue to make the wrong decisions, the more our heart hardens; the more often we make the right decision, the more our heart softens."

—ERICH FROMM, *THE HEART OF MAN*

"A series of little lies can eventually blur one's capacity to see moral distinctions about big things."

—CHARLES COLSON, *BORN AGAIN*

"Every time you make a choice you are turning the central part of you, the part of you that chooses, into something a little different from what it was before. And taking your life as a whole, with

all your innumerable choices, you are slowly turning this central thing either into a heavenly creature or into a hellish creature."

—C. S. LEWIS, *MERE CHRISTIANITY*

I suspected there was something wrong with my life, my sense of identity, and with me as a person. I was afraid to admit that my sense of self was all fake, and spiraled into a deep depression. In my reasoning, *any* sense of identity, no matter how ugly, was much better than *no* sense of identity. The books I read gave me encouragement to find my way. One evening when Donnie came by, I mustered up the courage to share my thoughts with him.

"I feel disgusted with myself, Donnie, and realize I have no true substance as a person. Everything about my image, reputation, and identity have been built to cast myself in a good light to others." He sat quietly and let me continue. "On the yard, I wanted to be known as a hustler. In the gang, my reputation was built on violence and loyalty. With my family and college professors, I wanted to be recognized as smart and capable. I'm a total fake, and I don't even know who the hell I am." I felt so lost.

Donnie, to his credit, gave me space to continue talking and did not interrupt or try to give advice. At the end of our session, a small spark of excitement settled over me. In talking things out loud, I realized I had a blank slate to resurrect a new identity if I wanted to.

One day, I sat in the dayroom with headphones on, my blue notebook open. I was in my own world, undisturbed. At a nearby table were a pile of discarded books. I looked them over, and the titles looked uninteresting. In the small stack was a Bible, and for some reason I felt moved to open it. Inside, I found words that gave me solace, inspiration, and most importantly, hope. There was a theme of casting off old selves in order to embrace the new. Over the years in prison, I randomly showed up in church here and there, but it always felt empty. That Sunday, I attended Mass and felt the power of the words for the first time in my life.

A whole new world opened up for me inside prison. Eventually in my search for knowledge, I became fascinated with books on the saints. They were all flawed in one way or another and yet were able to build something of their lives and leave lasting legacies. One of my favorites was Saint Francis of Assisi, born into a rich family of merchants. Despite his wealth, he was described as a rogue and a hedonist and was eventually imprisoned. One day, he encountered a man on the side of the road who had parts of his face and hands eaten away by leprosy, yet uncharacteristically embraced him with love and kindness. That is where his process of conversion began, as he walked away from riches and what the world saw as valuable. Saint Francis went on to found the Franciscan order.

I wished I could meet these spiritual heroes and pick their minds. At least I could glimpse their intimate thoughts by reading their writings, I reasoned. At that point, I wanted to salvage something of my life, despite my failures as a human being. This kindled the first spark of how I wanted to resurrect myself, even if I were to die in prison. Like Saint Francis, I could treat lepers around me with love and kindness. On the prison yard, we had our own lepers—men who were mentally challenged, socially outcast, or discarded as people not even worth talking to. In a way, I felt like a leper myself and only wanted to be embraced.

CHAPTER 8

THE SONG OF THE SPARROW

PRESIDING COMMISSIONER: In the file, we got a support letter from Donnie. This is a support letter?

INMATE HUYNH: Yes, sir.

PRESIDING COMMISSIONER: A good friend of yours.

INMATE HUYNH: Yes, he was actually a life-term inmate that was found suitable. We still keep in touch.

PRESIDING COMMISSIONER: What's he doing?

INMATE HUYNH: He is working down in San Diego the last he wrote me. He became my mentor for the last six months before he left, and he stayed in touch with me.

I looked forward to my meetings with Donnie. I shared with him what I discovered about myself for that week or something about a lesson in a book that I wanted to apply in my life. Of course, not everyone shared in our excitement. A lot of people began to scoff at me, and I heard that most people thought I had gone crazy. In my dorm, Success began to make snide comments about me trying to trick everyone into thinking I was trying to change and go home. Freddie would mutter under his breath about how none of us, especially me, could ever go home. Even Todd, the man who had connected me to Donnie in the first place, began to say that what Donnie was telling me was a sham.

They did not understand my excitement. I had discovered a way to find some sense of freedom in my life and, most particularly, my mind. One evening while Donnie and I were talking, he stopped, sat back, and pointed at me. "You can go home. I know a lot of people will doubt you, but I believe in you, Quan. I really think you can go into the board and demonstrate that you are a changed man one day." His kind words of support caused me to tear up even though I tried to hold them back. I felt self-conscious; it was weak to show emotions of any kind in prison. But Donnie was looking at me with such genuine kindness that I couldn't hold back the tears. I covered my face and wept at the table in the middle of the dayroom, hoping that nobody saw me. "Remember, Quan, you ain't ever got it unless you can give it back. I won't be here when you go to the board in a few years because I will be home by then. I want you to continue to give this back to as many men as possible in here." That night, I lay in my bed and sobbed tears of joy, happiness, and regret. The next morning, I woke up feeling much better and realized the tears had been healing. My life seemed to have new purpose.

Donnie went to the board later that month and was found suitable. A lifer found suitable still had to wait 120 days for review of the file to make sure the hearing was conducted properly and in accordance with state laws. If the lifer was in for murder, he then had to wait an additional thirty days for the case to go across the governor's desk. This is where every governor historically overturned the finding of suitability, and the lifer would have to go through the board hearing process all over again. Because of *In re Lawrence*, though, lifers who had been found suitable could file and sometimes find relief in the courts. Donnie, though, had been incarcerated for a kidnap/robbery, so the governor did not have to review his case. He was going to go home.

There were a couple of thousand men on each yard at Solano, the vast majority of them lifers. For years, it was referred to as the graveyard for life-term prisoners. Whenever anyone was found suitable, that person became a celebrity of sorts. People would point them out on the yard or in the chow hall and whisper about how they knew that person, almost as if proximity to someone who was found suitable would mean that they would get to go home one day, too. Donnie suddenly had a following of lifers who began to ask him all sorts of questions. During Donnie's weekly meetings with me, there were lots of men who came up to him to ask his advice, many of them the same ones who had doubted him. These men would hang on to every word that Donnie said even though he never told them what to say at the board.

On the other end of the spectrum, there were guys like Freddie and Todd. Freddie believed that Donnie had only been found suitable because he was in for a kidnap. I noticed him leaning against the wall near someone else's dorm muttering under his breath, and had the feeling he was saying something hypercritical of Donnie or even me. He had stopped coming by my bunk area to talk to me after Donnie was found suitable. Todd, the person who had introduced me to Donnie in the first place, had quit his weekly sessions with Donnie. He said Donnie's case did not apply to him because they were different circumstances.

Donnie reminded me, "These guys are looking for a get-out-of-jail-free card, Quan. And I don't have that for them. What we are talking about here is demonstrating that we take full responsibility for our actions, not only for the crimes we committed but our conduct in prison after."

Somewhere during our meetings, I realized we were no longer discussing the board, my poor self-concepts, or my lack of self-esteem. We were connecting and having a genuine, heartfelt friendship. We talked about his love for playing basketball; I spoke about mine for playing football. He told me about the pies that he would make for me one day when I came home, and I talked about introducing him to my family. We talked about things we would like to do when we were released. It no longer seemed imaginary to dream of going home. Shortly thereafter, Donnie was paroled. It was one of my happiest days during my life sentence.

One morning, I was called out for a medical appointment. I stood near one of the big mechanical gates that kept the individual yards separated from each other. A couple of men waited for the officer in the gun tower to open up the gate. I leaned on the fence, the razor wire above me. The morning was cold and crisp, and the sun started peeking over the nearby hills. My mind had that serene peacefulness that always came over me from prayer and meditation. I was thinking about how I could apply lessons from books I was reading in my life. The legacies of the saints were on my mind, and I thought to myself, why could I not also leave a legacy from in here, even if I am to die in prison? It dawned on me that I could; prison did not have to be this harsh ugly place of punishment but a place where I could remake myself. It was a subtle shift in my view of prison, but it was all the difference in the world. Suddenly, I felt the warmth from the sun radiate throughout my body, and I noticed the dew on the individual blades of grass. Up above me in the razor wire I heard the chirp of a sparrow. I looked up, and there it was, perched between the circular coils of the shiny razor wire. It was dark brown with uneven white streaks. I noticed it was missing the lower part of one leg and, on the other, had only three claws instead of four. It was obvious it had lost the claw and limb from landing on the razor wire. Yet, with all the scarring and deformities, the sparrow still perched proud, singing for whoever was listening.

A sense of inner joy washed over me. I then noticed signs of life all around me. Plants and flowers were in bloom. I breathed in the fresh smell of morning. Some kind of insects were buzzing around the fading light of a light pole, the same light poles that cast the eerie fluorescent yellow over every prison yard at nighttime. In the distance, I spotted a hawk circling, already on the hunt for the day. I looked up at the razor wire again, and a second sparrow had landed near the first one. This one was also scarred, with a lump where one of his claws used to be. They were both singing. *All these years they have been singing, and I have not been listening*, I thought to myself. I looked at the men nearby, and nobody seemed to notice anything. *None of us have been listening.*

From that day forth, prison did not feel like punishment anymore. It became a place where I could begin to remake myself into someone better. Every time I went out to the yard, I noticed the sparrows and listened to their songs. Each one of these sparrows were disfigured and scarred in so many ways, yet they were content and free. I wished the same for myself and for my soul.

I developed a habit of journaling that opened up my mind. My evening journals became a repository for my thoughts. I dumped everything into them, whatever I was thinking, feeling, and trying to incorporate into my life. I gained clarity over my own thoughts. In my journals, I learned to forgive myself. For example, I read books on mindfulness and meditation and others on effective communication. I noticed that many times during conversations with people, in my mind, I picked apart what they said. Instead of hearing them, I only wanted to prove people wrong. My mind had no filter, and I judged others harshly. The books I read challenged me to approach conversations in a different way.

In my journals each evening, I reviewed my day. I wrote down where I could improve in my interactions, how I could slow down my responses, and what to do moving forward. For example, one evening I was sitting on the concrete benches, feeding pigeons and sparrows with sunflower seeds from our lunch sacks. Another prisoner, Lefty, walked up near to where I sat and plopped down on the ground, startling the birds, and they flew away. He continued looking up at the sky.

"Didn't you see me trying to feed the birds here? Why did you just walk through here like that? You could have just walked around," I said, upset. Lefty was one of those prisoners we referred to as a J Cat, a person who should have been housed in a mental institution. He hardly showered, and most days he sat in the middle of the yard, staring up at the clouds.

"I'm sorry, man! I was watching the clouds! Look how pretty everything is!"

Lefty was right. Solano did have beautiful cloud formations at sunset that were painted pink and purple across the sky from the high winds. But that did not excuse him from not noticing anything else around him. Before I could cuss him out, though, Lefty uttered words that stick with me to this day:

"Somebody once told me every single moment is precious. Those clouds right now up there"—he pointed—"you will never ever see that formation again. Enjoy it while you can." With that, he stood up and walked away, looking at another cloud formation.

I felt like such an idiot. How could I hope to emulate Saint Francis when I had already judged a man like Lefty? He was our present-day leper, and I had failed once again. That evening, I made notes for myself to treat the next Lefty I encountered with patience and kindness.

Each new day was another learning lesson. Every difficult conversation, every challenging person to deal with, was an opportunity for me to practice the wisdom that I was trying to embody. I journaled each evening on different thoughts I had.

> Journal entry on giving to the community:
>
> *"Today, I understand the value of what my father was trying to teach me thirty-odd years ago about giving back wholeheartedly to my community. Saint Luke stated, "Much is expected from those to whom much is given." I believe I have been given much grace, and now try to share the light that has been kindled within me with everyone I come across in my path. Whereas in my past I only left a trail of death, pain, and destruction, today I hope to leave seeds of love and light in my footprints, and with God's help those seeds can bloom into something beautiful in this world."*

Journal entry on meditation:

"This budding benefit of meditation has helped to transform my world; I notice I am more discerning of my thoughts, of other people's words, and it is a way for me to gauge my own inner feelings. Many of the spiritual books I have read speak extensively about finding something special in the stillness of our hearts and what they term the interior life; I would like to say I have found a way to enrich my own."

Journal entry after reading about Mother Teresa:

"Most importantly, though, are the choices I make whenever I come across somebody on my path. Mother Teresa stated it best: 'Great acts done without love is nothing. Small, everyday acts done with great love is what life is all about.' I believe these small everyday acts done with great love must be accomplished by viewing every person I come across each day with eyes and thoughts that do not judge, label, or criticize. It is extremely difficult for me, but the rare moments when I have been able to simply accept and recognize the person in front of me as a divine creation of God, and can be there in that present moment, I have felt absolutely filled with joy, contentment, and peace."

Journal entry on choices:

"Today I have learned to recognize and celebrate my strengths but also realize that without a moral compass to make my decisions from, these same strengths can become glaring character flaws. For example, my ability to be creative and organize things is also the same ability to become devious and crafty. That is why I believe it is so crucial for me to continue to make the right choices every day. It was my small everyday choices that had diminished me as a person;

it is these same correct choices that will continue to transform me, I hope, into something beautiful for God one day."

Early one morning, I was watching the news on TV. I had finished my meditation and was in a quiet, reflective mood. The volume was off, and as I watched the words scroll across, I realized, *That's how my mind works when it comes to my thoughts! That's how all our minds work!* Except that instead of one feed, there were multiple feeds scrolling across at any given moment. Some scrolled faster than others, and some were louder or more pronounced. I was reading *The Unfettered Mind*, a collection of writings by the Zen master Takuan Soho, a Buddhist monk who had counseled and mentored the most famous ronin swordsman of his time, Miyamoto Musashi.

His teachings continued to expound on the value of removing clutter from the mind and to have no thoughts at all. It sounded completely contradictory, of course, until the revelation with the feed on the bottom of the news channel. When my mind was cluttered and jumbled with many thoughts, my decision-making process was erratic and rushed. But when I made time for meditation and found that inner sanctum of peace and contentment, with no thoughts intruding or racing through my head, my actions would flow more purposefully. I experienced something like a gentle glow of clarity with regard to the world and everyone I came across in those moments.

After that, I looked at my surroundings with a different perspective. I noticed the men around me, how they spoke to each other, and how they related to each other. I questioned the fabric of what we called prison life. In my journals, I explored my thought processes and how to refine them. I thought about the imprint I would like to leave on the world, even while in prison.

I noticed other small communities and groups who were trying to make the best of prison life, and I got involved with them.

I saw there were many people all around in my present community at Solano who were willing and capable of supporting and helping me. I spoke to some therapists, and through psychological group therapy, I recognized that I had some major psychological issues. The lies I had woven about myself formed an intricate web that was intertwined into the fabric of my thought process and personality. I finally awoke and began my journey toward self-awareness.

In late 2011, early 2012, I wrote out a personal mission statement for myself. At first, in my journals, they started out as affirmations, but one day I shaped them and titled it "Your Inner Jewel." I read it to myself every morning, and the words helped me set my intention for the day. They became the parameters for me to stay on my path and a reminder for me to continue to polish and refine each facet of myself:

Practice Mindfulness
Listen Twice as Much as You Speak
Find Today's Lesson in Today's Difficulty
Strive for Excellence in All That You Pursue
Everyone Is Also on a Journey—Learn from Them All
You Are Responsible for Every Thought and Word in This Life
Seek Balance and Discipline; There Is a Fine Line in Everything You Do
Listen for Your Voices of Ego and Pride and Continue to Remove Them
Mind, Body, Heart, and Soul—Contribute to Them Constantly
Leave Time Daily to Find Your Inner Voice and Trust in It
Effectiveness with People, Efficiency with Everything Else
Do Not Fear Failure; That Is the Only Path to Success
Accomplish Transformation through Your Choices
Remember That Perfection Is Not Possible
Speak with Kind, Gentle, Yet Firm Words
Never Compromise with Honesty
Give Thanks for Today
Laugh at Life

During that time, I got involved with a twelve-step program, a creative writing group, and joined several self-help groups, one in particular called the Alternatives to Violence Project. In AVP, I was able to practice concepts that were foreign to me, such as effective communication, giving feedback, and working on teams. In our workshops, I saw how we impacted the culture on the prison yard, from one of violence to one of communication, respect, and dignity for each other. I felt alive in a fulfilling way, and there was a deep sense of purpose to my existence. AVP supplemented my journey of self-discovery, and everything in my life started to feel like the universe had conspired to help me out all these years, but I had never recognized it.

It felt like I had been collecting pieces of a jigsaw puzzle through my experiences, with no idea of what the finished puzzle would look like or where each piece would fit. But now I had a glimpse of the picture, and my mind and heart saw the world with renewed clarity and purpose. I felt a compelling need to go back to Mass and reaffirmed my faith in the Catholic Church.

One of the self-help groups I joined focused on cognitive behavioral therapy. One of my assignments in cognitive behavioral therapy was to name two self-defeating thoughts that I was working on. Here is what I wrote in August 2011:

> *Two self-defeating thoughts I struggle with would have to be my perpetual sense of self-doubt and my fear of failure, closely related. I notice that I tend to overanalyze things and in the process find reasons why I might not accomplish certain tasks I set out to do and start doubting myself. This self-doubt usually creeps in after I am fully committed to something and I have passed the point of no return.*
>
> *For example, I recently facilitated an Alternatives to Violence Project (AVP) workshop and was leading a meditation exercise. In the middle of the reading, I started questioning myself. "Am I reading this at a reasonable pace? Am I using the right inflections at the proper moments? What if these guys don't connect? What if I stumble or stutter on the next sentence?" They all inevitably lead to my other self-defeating thought, "What if I fail?"*
>
> *It's a constant cycle that goes through my head. I recognize, though, that these self-defeating thoughts are unhealthy. I try to address them by always asking myself, "Did I try my best?" I know now not to view things in terms of black and white, right or wrong. Instead, I am starting to understand that growth is a continual process. The*

only way to do that is to push my limits, accept my failures and my triumphs, and not immobilize myself by obsessing over trivial thoughts. It is much easier said than done, but it is something I am working on.

In my creative writing group, I wrote again for the first time in twenty-plus years. Writing creatively was healing for me, and it opened the door for me to explore my father's death. One day, I wrote a long letter to him while lying on my bunk. I cried while writing it and hoped that nobody saw me. It ended up being about two pages long, and I expressed a lot of things I was never able to tell him before and after his death. I saw a therapist monthly and brought in the letter during our next session. She agreed to listen as I read it, and I choked and sobbed throughout the reading, a mixture of snot and tears running down my face. I wept for my father for the first time in my life and did not care that somebody saw me. Writing the letter was therapeutic, but reading it out loud was the catalyst for deep healing. It helped mend the scars.

That evening, I let it all go. I tore the letter up and flushed it down the toilet. Unlike my mourning cloth, though, this act was done with forgiveness and understanding, not anger and shame. Once I began to come to terms with my father's death and how profoundly it had affected me, I recognized the grieving process all around me. Elisabeth Kübler-Ross's book, *On Death and Dying*, gave me a great framework to notice what she coined the Five Stages of Grief when it comes to loss. I started to see it in the other men around me. Many of them had lost parents, siblings, wives, or girlfriends along the way.

A man could still go through the different stages even if he did not experience the death of a loved one. In prison, men experienced a similar loss when they were denied at the board over and over, when a significant other or family member stopped communicating, or when they were uprooted and transferred from one prison to another. Growing old in prison was a loss. All the men around me had experienced many sorts of loss during their incarceration. None of them had any way of processing or grieving them.

I drafted a curriculum, crafted how the groups would run, complete with prompts, facilitated questions, and a twelve-week agenda. I approached one of the psychologists on the yard and shared with him what I had created. He loved it, and within several weeks, we had launched the prison's first ever Grief and Loss group. The waiting list was long, as we could serve only a dozen men at a time.

About halfway through our first cohort, the psychologist was transferred to a different prison. Without a staff sponsor, the group could no longer come together until we had another prison official who agreed to sit in on our groups and sign off on it. I was sad; it was important to get the group recognized so men had a space to process their losses. One of the participants worked in the program office, and he had a lot of connections with other staff sponsors. He thought he could find a sponsor for us, so I shared with him the course outline and syllabus that I had put together. Nothing ever came of it, though.

Several months later, I saw a sign-up sheet in my building. There, along the top in bold were the words *Grief and Loss.* I felt sick to my stomach as I realized the participant had submitted my syllabus as his own! *How could I have trusted this dude?* I was disgusted with myself. *The audacity of this fool! How could he blatantly steal my work and think that I would let it go? He must think I am a coward! Who the hell was this idiot anyway? Some guy who came in for killing his wife and still hasn't accepted any type of responsibility for it.* My thoughts spiraled as I plotted ways to get him. I wanted to stab him or cut his throat. I knew if I did something, he would tell on me. *What if I caught him slipping where there were no cops around? What if I waited until we had a group together and follow him out into the restrooms and attack him while he urinated? Could I knock him out and stomp on his head so that he would not recall what happened? Would I get away with this? Would there be witnesses?* Then another sobering thought: *How could I still think these thoughts if I had sworn to walk a path of nonviolence?*

Whenever I was upset or frustrated about something, I processed it in my journal. That night I wrote, and raged, and asked myself some hard questions. What was my purpose in creating the group? If it was to help other men, what did it matter if my name was attached to it or not? What did it say about me that I felt I should be recognized as the creator of the group? The thief, in his way, was still helping other men to process their losses, and that is all that should matter. It was a sobering pill to swallow, but I decided to let it all go. I noticed that the man no longer occupied any space in my mind, and I was able to regain power and focus my energy on more positive aspects for myself and the community.

Shortly thereafter, I was interviewed by National Public Radio. My immediate supervisor had recommended me so that I could highlight how we made prison a better place by the self-help groups we created.

We were in the middle of the yard. I sat on one of the concrete benches. The woman held a long skinny mic connected by a thin wire to what I assumed was her recorder, a small black box about the size of a deck of cards. It was a warm day, but she wore a thick brown coat. She kept it buttoned all the way up, perhaps to protect her from the stares of nearby prisoners. She was attractive, and the men were looking—not only because of her beauty, but also because we did not have outside guests every day with microphones and radio equipment. My supervisor stood to the side with a couple of correctional officers but could still hear everything we said.

The interview was going well, I could tell. She was impressed with what we had been up to and even more fascinated about my motivations for creating the Grief and Loss group. I shared with her how I collaborated with a psychologist after I saw there was a common problem on the yard. I also let her know I facilitated the Victims Awareness group on the yard, where we got men to realize the harm that they caused to those around them. As I talked with her, I felt she saw me as a human being and not a prisoner. I felt good inside and maybe even likable, smart, and charismatic. I imagined she was even enthralled by my charming smile because she was also smiling at me. That was until she asked about my background.

"How long have you been in now?" she asked.

I gulped. "Thirteen years."

I saw her eyes widen and her mouth parted ever so slightly. "How much longer do you have to do?"

"I have a life sentence, ma'am. I will be going to my first parole hearing at the end of next year."

Her eyes opened even more. "And what are you in prison for?" The question trailed off.

Up until that moment, whenever someone asked, I would answer that I was in prison for a gang-related murder. I would always be sure to emphasize the gang-related. That way, they knew I was in a gang, which would help to establish my place in the prison hierarchy right off the bat. It would also alleviate any fears I had of anyone judging me because I wanted to be somebody respected and liked.

More recently, though, because of my involvement in the Victims Awareness groups, I had a deep feeling of remorse regarding my murder. I did not view this as a badge of honor, and in my journal the previous week, I had challenged myself to get away from diminishing my victim by referring to my case as a gang-related murder.

I breathed in and looked up at her light brown eyes. "I am in prison for the murder of another human being." My heart began to race, and time seemed to slow. Everything in me, even though I was intentional about what came out of my mouth, wanted to justify or explain. She had withdrawn from the interview, and I could tell she was waiting for me to explain. In fact, everything in me wanted her to ask me to explain so I could be relieved of this internal struggle and get her to like and connect with me again.

What if she thinks I went to prison for killing a woman, like my ex-girlfriend or something? What if she thinks I am some crazy serial killer? All these what-ifs started going through my mind, but I gently pushed them to the side. Instead, I continued focusing on my breath. I still looked at the interviewer and noticed the officers and my supervisor shifted on their feet. I am in prison for the murder of another human being. That's the bottom line. But I am no longer that person. Yet, my truth makes people uncomfortable. The longer I sat still, the more I felt a sense of calm power wash over me, a strange sense of liberation, of not being tethered to a certain identity or expectation from others. I realized I was OK with what I had said and did not need to explain any further.

We ended the interview after that. She did not say anything else except a quick "Thank you for your time." I saw that something had also shifted inside her. Whether good or bad, I will never know. I realized I was finally starting to accept myself, even with all my faults. The sparrows never explained their deformities and only sang for whoever listened. I would never again give a disclaimer for why I was in prison.

CHAPTER 9

THE MONSTER INSIDE

PRESIDING COMMISSIONER: So what contributions do you think you've made to society, if any?

INMATE HUYNH: Recently, we did a polar plunge for the Special Olympics children of Northern California. I was part of the Peer Health team to help organize and give money back. They selected me to lead the training workshop in two weeks, and I'm going to be able to be part of a team to help train new men as AVP facilitators to help pass our message of peace and nonviolence. I hear guys all the time, like even in Victims Awareness when I facilitate it, well, I want to do this when I go home, and I challenge them, why do you want to wait until you go home; why can't it start here? I think the lifestyle starts here; the change starts here so that when you go home you're already doing it. And that's what I believe I'm trying to make for myself and make for others while we're here in this community.

PRESIDING COMMISSIONER: All right.

INMATE HUYNH: It's literally transformed my world from within here. I'm contributing something of value for once in the world. I'm doing something meaningful. I can be recognized but in a fulfilling type of way where it's enriching to my soul. It's not about the competitive part of my nature, the ugly part of me that wants to be number one. It's a different part—that I've been able to develop and to nurture within myself like, 'Hey, I feel good inside for once.' I have—I found true happiness and I don't need a great title. I don't need a—to make a lot of money. I don't need any of this. It's just something like—I love to do, so that's the only way I can describe it.

PRESIDING COMMISSIONER: All right, sir.

By 2011, a couple of years before my Initial Parole Consideration Hearing, I busied myself with understanding the board process. Most men did not share their transcripts, but I had gotten a glimpse of Alabama's back in 2007. I knew there was so much knowledge to be learned in the failures of others.

Brian Tracy's book *Change Your Thinking, Change Your Life* had me thinking of what he had coined *inverse paranoid*. It is a person who is convinced that the world is conspiring to make him or her a better person. I loved that way of thinking and saw many examples every day of the universe conspiring to help me out. I realized that prison, and in essence my life sentence, could be viewed as a way to make me into a better person. I saw around me people who were paranoid, who believed the world had conspired to screw them over. I did not want to become bitter and resentful like them. Instead, I began to look at my surroundings with positive suspicion. A game I liked to play was trying to discover who would cross my path that day to help me out on my journey.

There was a guy named Bobby on the yard who lived in my building. He was thin of build and in his late fifties, with thick glasses and a small mustache. Although he worked in the optical lens lab, he still continued to wear the same pair of glasses that he most likely had during his arrest in the early '80s. One of the arms was wrapped up with some medical tape, causing the glasses to sit on his long pointy nose a little askew. He was quiet and kept to himself. Our friendship began over our mutual interest in books. Bobby had this habit of leaving a book square in the middle of my bed whenever he finished one or was returning one that he had borrowed from me. On top of the book, there would be a pack of the prison-issued chocolate chip cookies. They had plastic wrapping and were stale and tough to bite into. Most men dipped them into cold milk to soften them up. I loved to bite into mine and let the piece soften in my mouth while I read my books.

Bobby went out of his way to please everyone. Unfortunately, a lot of guys preyed on his kindness. Bobby was paid seventy-five cents an hour, one of the highest pay rates one could achieve while in prison. So he always had money to buy extra food from the canteen, such as chips, cookies, and meat sausages. The same two or three guys would ask to borrow food from him every month, but they never repaid him. Of course, this was none of my business since he was a different race. He reminded me of a loyal dog. Even when it gets kicked, it will come back, happy and wagging its tail.

Bobby had been to the parole board at least eight times. In the course of our friendship, he opened up to me, and one day in our conversation he offered to let me read his transcripts. I saw a pattern in the hearings. During a typical hearing, the commissioner always stated on the record that they were not there to retry the case. They made sure Bobby understood they were there only to determine his suitability for parole. I found it odd that they always stated this at the beginning of every hearing. Later, I realized this was the key to everything.

According to the transcripts, Bobby had killed his wife by stabbing her to death. She had been verbally abusive and left him numerous times but always came back after several months. He never had any run-ins with the law before. One day, he had stabbed her to death in their kitchen. He swore to me that he had accepted responsibility, but when I read his transcripts, it did not look that way.

Every time the commissioners asked about the sequence of events before the murder, Bobby insisted there was a shadow that had startled him. He stated he had grabbed a nearby knife and stabbed at it, and it was his wife. Throughout his whole prison sentence, he was a model inmate and did not get into any type of trouble. But in reading the transcripts, it dawned on me why the board was not finding him suitable: he was not accepting full responsibility for his actions. He continued to cast himself in a good light, especially when speaking about his darkest moments as a human being. I noticed it took away from his authenticity and the Bobby that I knew. In the hearings, when the commissioners denied parole to Bobby, they outlined several reasons, the same reasons I had noted when I read the transcripts.

The theme was similar over the course of eight different transcripts that I read. After reading them, I still did not understand what caused Bobby to stab his wife to death, and more importantly, I did not feel Bobby did either. Donnie's words of wisdom continued to resonate with me: "You ain't got it unless you give it back." I knew that I could help Bobby, but I was unsure how.

One evening, as we were sitting in the dayroom together, we began talking about one of the books I had shared with him recently, *Sensible Self-Help*. We were discussing one of the terms in there, *self-responsibility*. In essence, it was the understanding and acceptance of the fact that it was our interpretations, and not outer circumstances, that determined our ability to respond to people, situations, our feelings, our awareness of choices available, and ultimately our behavior. It was my subtle hint to Bobby that he needed to learn some self-responsibility. Since I was practicing these concepts for about a year now, in my arrogance, I figured I could teach it to him.

The next morning, though, I learned my own lessons from the most unlikely teacher. The morning call for breakfast was announced over the PA system, and the men gathered in front of their dorms. I noticed quite a few of the men were wearing their bright yellow raincoats. The raincoats were heavy and hot and smelled of mildew. I walked up to the top tier, looked out the windows, and saw the yellow reflection of the prison floodlights on the damp concrete; the rain had stopped. I decided not to grab my raincoat.

The familiar "click, click" of the officer pressing the button on the PA system signaled our release for breakfast. Like everyone else, I wanted to beat most of the crowd, so I shuffled to the front of the line and through the sally port. The whispers of the men talking early in the morning, before sunrise, was comforting. It reminded me of how my father and I had spoken quietly during our early morning road trips. As we walked along the sidewalk toward the chow hall, the blaring of an alarm stopped us all in our tracks.

"Get down!! Get down!!" Correctional officers ran toward one of the buildings, and as I started to sit down, I realized the ground was wet. Instead, I squatted, while keeping an eye on my surroundings. *Why do I always think of the worst-case sce-*

nario when an alarm goes off? I thought. Other men who did not have raincoats on around me also squatted to avoid getting damp. Men in rain jackets had plopped onto the small puddles of water in the concrete.

Most of the time, alarms sounded because one of the prisoners had a medical issue. Other times, though, it was because of a fight or, even worse, a race riot. I continued to watch my surroundings. A medical golf cart began to make its way across the yard toward the same building the officers had run into, and the tension left my body. The golf cart signaled a medical issue.

"Get down on the ground!" a gruff voice barked. It was one of the correctional officers. He stomped up to where we were crouched on the ground. He had a light green rain jacket over his dark green uniform, and I recognized him as Officer Stanley. He was a stickler for the rules, and I knew he would not hesitate to harass or write us up if we did not sit down. I saw an area of concrete that did not have a puddle, slid over, and sat down. I felt the cold dampness seeping into my pants and boxers. I became irritated with Stanley. Other men around me were grumbling, and I could feel the tension of hatred and anger directed toward him. Officer Stanley walked up to a nearby man who was still squatting on his haunches. "Do you want to sit down, or do you want me to lay you on that ground?"

The other man pleaded with Stanley. "But it's wet, Stanley. You know there's no fight over there. It's only a medical issue."

"I don't give a fuck what it is. The alarm went off; you are to be sitting on that ground!" He pointed, and the man sat down into a puddle of water. At that moment, the skies opened up, and rain began coming down. I felt my body becoming tense and I glared at Stanley. *This guy is such an idiot. I am getting soaking wet because of him!*

Nearby, I heard someone giggling with joy, and it didn't make sense. I looked over and it was Bobby, with the most serene smile on his face. He was dripping wet, drops of rain on the edge of his nose and on the tips of his mustache. His wet clothes clung to his body.

He started laughing again, then whispered to me, "Self-responsibility! We should have grabbed our rain jackets! This is what the book said!" He then looked up at the sky, and the rain continued to caress his face. He looked back over at me and smiled. It was the most gentle, heartwarming smile.

I realized I had a choice in all this. I could choose to be angry at myself for not grabbing the raincoat. I could choose to be angry at Stanley for making us sit down. I could choose a million different thoughts that would further taint how my day would start. Instead, I decided to choose to let it all go and consciously chose to enjoy that moment, sitting in the rain with no raincoat on. When the officers let us all back up, everyone quickly walked to the chow hall. Bobby and I, without even talking about it, were the last ones to walk in. Here I was, thinking I was the one helping Bobby, but he had given me the gift of a lifetime with one simple smile and a lesson about choice in the rain. I could still choose happiness, even with a storm of thoughts raging through me.

Several days later, we sat across from each other at one of the dayroom tables. In Bobby's transcripts, I used yellow post-it notes to point out areas that I felt we needed to address. In each of his transcripts I saw one common thread—an inability to accept complete responsibility for his actions. Bobby would admit to stabbing his wife, but then in the next sentence he would say something like, "But I didn't mean it," or "It was only an accident," or "But it wasn't intentional." In reading his transcripts, this is where I felt Bobby lacked any understanding of his motivations the day of his murder. Instead, he had told himself a script over the years, and this became such a core part of his identity. It came out in every hearing. I shared with him my thoughts and pointed out to him where I saw the issue. He seemed receptive, but I was determined to make sure that he did not make that mistake again in the boardroom.

Donnie had taught me the power of sitting across from someone and looking them in the eye while they spoke. Bobby continued to shift in his chair as I threw questions at him. I definitely did not know what I was asking, but with my notes from the transcripts, I began to find my way. This became a weekly ritual of ours, where we would sit at a dayroom table and do our mock hearings. Of course, since we lived in a fishbowl of sorts, everyone soon knew that I was trying to help Bobby prepare for the board. People scoffed, and Bobby was asked the simple question, "How can Quan help you prepare for the board when he has never even been to one?"

The men began to whisper that I was crazy to think that I could ever help anyone or to think that I could go home. They were right, of course, until I realized they were wrong. The more Bobby and I sat, the more I realized that humans wanted to portray their best selves. Bobby's main issue came down to facing why he had stabbed his wife to death. In not wanting to face it, there were certain words that came out in the way he described it. One evening in one of our exchanges, Bobby insisted once again that he saw a shadow.

"Bobby, there was no shadow." We were sitting at a table in the middle of a crowded dayroom. Everyone around us was doing their regular prison routines: working out, playing chess, dom-inoes, or pinochle. However, all I saw was Bobby seated across from me.

He looked up at me and said, "Yes, there was, Quan. I am telling you, that is what startled me."

"Bobby, I am your friend. Do you trust me enough to listen to what I am saying? I am telling you, this is why the board is not finding you suitable. Remember, we talk about self-responsibility and how we are trying to practice it. How can you say that you accept responsibility and yet blame it on a shadow? Do you hear yourself?"

"I am not blaming it on a shadow! I did stab Elizabeth! But there was a shadow before it happened!" His hands gripped the table, and he glared at me.

Listening to the words that come forth from someone else's mouth gives me a good glimpse of how they see the world. I realized this is what Bobby believed. He had told himself this story for so many years, and it had become ingrained into the fabric of his thoughts. It was now part of his self-concept and identity, and to admit to himself a part of his identity was fake was, in his mind, terrifying for him. I understood that. I had been there. *I wonder what parts of my own identity are still fake?* I pushed the nagging thought away.

"OK, Bobby. Tell me what was going on leading up to that day."

Bobby told me the same story he had shared previously. He

and his wife constantly argued. She was verbally and emotionally abusive, would leave him, come back, and Bobby would accept her with open arms. Whenever Bobby spoke about the dynamics with his ex-wife, in both his transcripts and with me, he always blamed himself for why she became angry. He continued to blame himself for her leaving him. Bobby then dropped a bombshell on me.

"After the last time she left me, I thought it was over. But a few months after, she came back and told me she was pregnant with our kid!" Bobby smiled but did not look happy.

"Bobby! How come you never spoke about this before?"

"Because she was pregnant with our child!" He then grabbed the white handkerchief that he always carried, removed his glasses, and wiped his eyes. He looked back up at me. "I killed two people that day, and nobody knows!" Bobby began to cry while looking like he was laughing. He set his glasses back on, and his voice became a monotone as he looked up at me. "We already had names on what we were going to name our child. I thought everything was finally OK with us. Then that day in the kitchen, we started arguing again. I don't remember what it was about, but just like all the other times, I wish I didn't make her mad. If that hadn't happened, she wouldn't have said what she said." Bobby was still looking at me.

"What…what did she say?" I leaned forward and saw Bobby for the first time in a new light. Here was a man who had been abused for so long. It still happened to him in prison. He still blamed himself for every conflict that happened and still had the same pattern of wanting to please the other person.

"She told me the child was not mine," he whispered. "I felt so angry and betrayed. I always suspected she might be cheating on me, but I never dared to ask in case she would yell at me. So for her to throw it in my face like that..." He put both hands over his face and sat still. I could feel my heart thumping in my chest. He folded one hand over another and put his chin on his hands while staring at me. "There was no shadow. I was so angry, and I had pushed everything away for so long. I grabbed the kitchen knife and stabbed her. I stabbed her over and over. There was so much blood. And once I started, I couldn't stop." Bobby took out his handkerchief and wiped his nose. He leaned forward and whispered, "The monster is still there, inside." He was pointing to the temple of his head. "The monster is there. The guys around here don't know that. Nobody knows that." He began to cry and laugh again, then stopped.

I did not know what to say, and everything in me wanted to fill up the uncomfortable silence in the loud dayroom with something. But I could only clear my throat.

"I am ready to come clean and let the board know the absolute truth." He breathed deeply, and there was a new resolve and brightness to his eyes. "There was no shadow, Quan. I have been lying all these years to everyone, especially myself. This is part of my journey of taking responsibility, and I am finally ready to do it from here on out."

Inside, I was leaping for joy for Bobby. At that moment, I knew that Bobby was going to be able to demonstrate that he was suitable. From reading his transcripts, I could tell the board only wanted him to accept complete and total responsibility, without blaming it on the shadow or any other external factors. Bobby was finally ready, and although I had never been in a board hearing, I knew in my heart the board was going to have a favorable ruling for him.

Bobby's hearing was still a couple of months away, but for those next two months, Bobby was a changed man. He walked with more purpose each day, and each evening he would come by my bunk area with a new thought he wanted to share.

That same week, another man came up to me and asked if I could help him prepare for the board. His name was Gee, and he was one of the fellow Asians on the yard. He had been to the board twice already. I told him I would only agree if he gave me his hearing transcripts. At first, he was hesitant but then finally relented and gave them to me. He was actually due to go the week before Bobby, and we started sitting down each evening. Gee had actually sat with Donnie before and was much further along than Bobby. As we began to go through his transcripts, I shared the same concepts of self-responsibility with him.

Gee was in for a gang-related murder. He and his homeboys had seen their rivals at a nearby park. When they pulled up next to the rival gang's car, Gee aimed his weapon to fire, but the gun had jammed. His rivals, in their panic, had jumped out of their car and run, and Gee's homeboys in a different car gunned them down. One person died, and one was injured. Everyone was convicted of murder and sentenced to fifteen years to life.

In his transcripts, although he admitted to being there, he still cast himself in a good light and did not accept complete responsibility. I pointed this out to him, and although he agreed, he was terrified of what coming clean meant. "I have told them for two hearings that I did not pull the trigger, which I did not. Now I am going to go in there and admit that I had intended to, and the only thing that prevented it from happening was my gun jammed. Dude, are you sure this is what I am supposed to do?"

I was unsure myself, but I did not let Gee know that. It felt right in my gut, though, and that is what I went with. Of course a part of me questioned my own motives. Gee would be testing my theory, and it was his life and freedom on the line, not mine. Whatever happened to him, I would learn and apply to my own hearing, which was still over two years away. I shared with Gee my own dilemma of taking complete responsibility at the board. The trial court had found me not guilty as the shooter. In reading every transcript, though, every commissioner stated on the record that they were not there to retry the case.

There were two options for me. One was to go into the hearing and give the same story I had given on the stand, that I was not the shooter, and blame it on the person who had turned state's evidence. It felt much safer that way. I definitely did not want the people who were going to decide my fate to think the worst of me, that I somehow had gotten away with my crime. Logic told me the commissioners would deny me parole on that alone, and I should never tell them the whole truth.

The other option for me was to go in and confess it all, let them know that I had lied on the stand, let them know that I was the shooter, and own up to everything. The choice of personal responsibility felt in alignment with everything I was reading. This option felt right in my gut even though it was terrifying in my mind to have to own up to it. Yet, in Gee's case, it was obvious to me that that was what he was supposed to do. When Gee told me I should own up to it, I realized we had the answer to each other's dilemmas. I decided then and there that when I walked into that hearing in a little over two years, I would hold myself accountable for all of my crimes, no matter what the board thought.

During our weekly meetings, we shared perspectives on our gang lifestyles. One of the things we both discovered were the similar reasons each of us felt compelled to join a gang. In listening to Gee's story, I realized I had the same insecurities of fitting in, a poor sense of self-identity and self-worth, and a need to be recognized and liked. Part of the allure of the gang life was the ready-made purpose by having enemies to fight. Being in the gang with the constant gang wars gave us an excuse to push everything else to the side, and that is why I never resolved any of the other issues in my life at the time. Each of us was a broken child with an overwhelming need to fit in. Over the years, with our experiences, we became hardened and cold to the outside. During our talks, I felt such a loss for my true self-identity, having hidden behind the warped sense of self that I developed as a gang member. I learned so much more from Gee during this time than he learned from me.

This newfound perspective and understanding began to give me a stronger foundation in which to live out each day on the yard. I did not feel like I had to defend myself or my sense of identity. The whispers that I had gone crazy began to bother me less, and I no longer felt the need to explain or show anyone that they were wrong and that I was right. This became more a path of trying to find my own sense of self-identity in the world, even if I had to go back and rebuild it all. I also felt an overwhelming sense of freedom inside. I was no longer tethered to anyone else's expectations of me and who I was supposed to be. It almost became an amusing secret; I was viewing the world with a different lens than I had been looking through all those years. I still inhabited the shell of my old self, but inside my mind, I saw the world with renewed clarity and purpose.

The weeks went by, and I learned more about myself each day that I sat with Gee. We knew that everyone in the building thought we were crazy, yet Gee and I both joked that it was everyone else who was crazy. We had discovered the secret to inner freedom, and no matter how we tried to share it, nobody was listening. It felt unfair that nobody wanted to hear about it.

On the day of Gee's hearing, I waited around nervously. I had stir fried some Chinese sausages with onions and bell peppers over a bed of rice for lunch and had made Gee a bowl. Parole hearings lasted anywhere from four to six hours, so I knew he would be hungry.

I sat at one of the dayroom tables when Gee walked through the sally port during the afternoon shift change of officers. He carried a small manila folder and had the biggest smile on his face.

"They found me suitable!" he screamed in the building. This caused an uproar, and men surrounded him. Others stood around and looked. I sat still, and my eyes blurred from the tears. We were right! This is what the board is looking for! They are human beings, and they only want to hear our stories and make sure that we are humans again.

It took over ten minutes for Gee to finally be able to make his way over to the table where I was sitting. We hugged each other tightly, and he sat down at the table. He opened the lid on the Tupperware bowl that I had put his lunch in, grabbed the sriracha bottle, and squeezed on a large red layer of the spicy sauce. He shoveled the food in his mouth.

"Homie, it's everything we talked about," he said between bites. His shaved head glistened with sweat from the spicy food. "They asked about my responsibility, and I let them know about the gun not working and that I intended to kill everyone." He grabbed an apple and took a bite of it, as he always did, to take the edge off the spice. He shoveled a couple more spoons of the food into his mouth, then grabbed a napkin to wipe the top of his head; it came away damp. "Thanks for the food; this was perfect, homie! Let's talk later. I gotta call my wife and then shower." He bit into the apple and held it in his mouth while picking up his folder and bowl.

"Here, leave the bowl. I got it. Go call your wife," I insisted.

Of course he refused. He mumbled something with the apple still in his mouth and shook his head. He grabbed the bowl to wash it and walked up the stairs toward his dorm. I noticed Bobby waiting at the top of the stairs, and both men embraced. Then Bobby looked over at me, smiled, and walked toward me.

"I'm ready to go in there and take responsibility for everything! I can't wait to go next week!" Bobby proclaimed as he sat down. "I'm ready!"

"Are you going to be ready tonight? Gee and I can go through some last stuff with you if you need to." Bobby was more than ready, but I felt it would be good to spend time with both him and Gee.

"No, I should rest between now and then. Things are going to be fine!" He took off his glasses, wiped them with his T-shirt, and put them back on.

During the next week while awaiting Bobby's hearing, several men came up to both Gee and me to help them prepare for the board. Yet some of them, in my mind, were not yet ready. They still did not accept full responsibility for their crimes. I noticed the common thing was for each person to say, "I accept full responsibility..." and then the next word would be "but," "just," "only," or something like that. It diminished everything that had preceded it. What was the point of owning up to something and then making an excuse about it? Yet, I noticed it happened often. Even in my daily conversations, the tendency to justify my mistakes or faults was a constant struggle. What better way to embody self-responsibility than to use my current circumstances as a training opportunity?

Bobby's hearing date came. Gee was still in his 150-day waiting period before his release. We sat at one of the dayroom tables, sorting through some of his paperwork. He had made some of his special burritos, and we had a few waiting for Bobby. It was early evening when Bobby walked into the building. His head was down, and he walked straight up the stairs to his dorm. He refused to talk to anyone. The buildings at Solano were like an open fishbowl, and we all knew that walk. Bobby had been denied parole.

My stomach started churning, and I found myself asking what Bobby had done wrong. He must not have accepted responsibility. Did he stumble about the shadow again? Maybe the commissioners wanted to deny him because he finally confessed about the pregnancy of his wife? I was quite confused.

Several minutes later, Bobby came back out of the dorm and made his way to the upstairs shower. He was in his white prison-issued boxers and was carrying a plastic soapbox and washcloth. From where Gee and I sat, we could see the low partition wall of the shower. The showers held four people at a time, but I saw only one towel there, which meant Bobby was in the shower by himself.

"Let's go up there and see what happened with him," I said.

Gee agreed, and we walked up to the shower area. It was normal for men to talk to each other while they were in the showers. Common courtesy dictated that the person outside the shower would turn his back to the people showering. This would prevent them from being accused of "peter gazing," our slang for looking at another man's privates. One of the first things I noticed as I approached the shower wall was Bobby's towel, neatly folded, with his old glasses set square right in the middle. From where I stood, I could still see the medical tape that held the arm to the temple.

Gee and I turned our backs to Bobby and leaned against the shower wall, with our elbows propped on the top part of it.

"What happened in there, Bobby? Why did they deny you? What did you say?" I asked him in quick succession. Only the sound of water hitting the floor of the shower answered me.

Gee nudged me and then simply said, "Bobby, how are you feeling?"

I felt so stupid. My questions, and the way I asked them, did nothing but blame Bobby for how the hearing went. Gee, instead, showed Bobby his support. *Another thing to add in my journal tonight and another thing to practice from here on out*, I thought. The books I was reading talked about the power of words and language and how they could build someone up or tear someone down. If I want to leave an imprint of goodness in the world, I need to do a better job of building people up.

"I feel terrible and confused," Bobby finally answered. "They denied me for another five years. I did everything we talked about. I took full and complete responsibility, and they still denied me. I don't think I will ever go home. Looks like I will die in here. I don't want to go to any more hearings. You guys don't know how bad it was in there."

I fought the urge to ask more questions about the hearing but instead took a page out of Gee's book and stayed silent. This allowed Bobby to continue. "They attacked me about my unborn child. I never should have told them about it! I went in there and took personal responsibility, and it didn't work! Gee, they gave you a date because you didn't actually kill anyone! Quan, if you go in there and admit to yours, they will never let you go home!"

I felt the familiar feelings of self-doubt wash over me again. We messed up. It wasn't this easy to go in there and get a date. What to do now? What was I thinking? Who was I to think I could look at this problem and solve it? What if he was right? Maybe Gee did get a date only because he didn't do it? There was another part of me, though, that felt this was still right, regardless if we were found suitable or not. Gee also looked confused.

Gee turned to me as we walked away. "The only way we'll know is when we read those transcripts, dog." I nodded in agreement.

The next few weeks became quite a blur because there were several men that I had agreed to help prepare for the board. One thing I mandated was that they had to provide me with their transcripts. There were quite a few that I had turned away, and one in particular, Rock, had become quite angry with me. Gee instead had agreed to help him, and I noticed they began to sit down often.

These coaching sessions with other prisoners became quite fascinating for me. Their agenda in sitting with me was to be found suitable. Pure and simple. I knew that, and although I wanted to help them, I knew it was not some magic combination of words that would get them out but more so a shift in mindset. I wanted a way to share with them how I already began to feel free at that moment, yet my own board hearing was still over two years away. It was hard to describe or convey to them. These were men who had been in close to twice as many years as me. Their experiences during those years had shaped the way they saw and perceived the world. Who was I to dismiss that and tell them what to do? There was always that sense of self-doubt inside me.

Yet, it always came down to the words they used and how they described their experiences. Listening to them gave me an intimate glimpse of how their mind and heart still experienced everything. Many times, I got the feeling these were men who had not accepted their faults yet, which then in turn got me to start thinking about the words I used to describe the world as I perceived it. My hearing was a couple of years away, and I knew I had a chance to continue to learn from these men as I helped them. Yet, something else also happened. I started to see how these words and the avoidance of accepting blame and fault for anything restricted these men from being their best selves. I wanted to try and become my best self.

Since his hearing, Bobby had withdrawn and did not come by my bunk area. I had tried to get him to open up to me, but it did not work. He did not want to discuss his hearing any further, and I was still confused about what had gone wrong in there. Little did I know that I would never sit down with Bobby ever again.

One day, as I was doing dips on the yard, Gee came up to me, fuming. He had been helping Rock for at least two to three hours every night. "Let me get some sets in with you, homie." He lifted himself on the dip bars and began doing his reps.

"What's wrong?" I asked.

"I should have listened to you! You had told me it was a waste of time to try and help them without transcripts, and now I see why. It's like I was going in there blind and don't even know where to start. I wasted all this time trying to help him and come to find out Rock was the trigger man! He tried to tell me this whole time that he wasn't, but he finally let me read his transcripts earlier. The commissioner read it into the record!" Gee did another two reps, started struggling on his way down for his third rep, and hopped off the bars. "All that time down the drain!" He clapped his hands together to remove the dust from the bars.

We finished our workout routine and then headed into the building to get showered and cleaned up. I walked up the stairs to my dorm. There, placed right in the middle of the gray wool blanket of my bed, was a burgundy transcript with one cookie pack on top of it. Without even looking, I knew it was Bobby's transcripts. I grabbed the transcript and started skimming through the pages to get a feel for how the hearing went. It seemed to be going fine, with Bobby expressing himself well at first. He shared about the pregnancy of his ex-wife. When the commissioners asked him why he did not disclose this at previous hearings, he started to make small, subtle excuses. Nothing major at first but justifications, nonetheless. Then the commissioners began to press Bobby on the actual murder.

Bobby disclosed that his wife had told him that the child was not his. The words that came out next made me realize forever how hard it was to speak the absolute truth at all times. I was in absolute shock as I read the words and had to reread the statement to make sure. There, right when asked what happened next, Bobby stated in the transcripts, "There was a shadow."

My mind spun, and I wanted to scream. I put the transcript down in disgust and had such an overwhelming sense of despair and sadness, mixed with anger and fear. It was easy to judge Bobby, yet I knew the fear of what he had faced in there was real. I was angry at Bobby because I felt that had he owned up to his crime completely, the commissioners would have found him suitable. But there was another part of me that was still unsure. I knew that my motivations in wanting him to say it were also selfish in nature, which caused me to become angry with myself.

I brought the transcripts over to Bobby's bunk area. I wanted to yell at him and scream at him for still talking about the shadow. I wanted him to admit to me that he was wrong and to apologize for lying to us that he had accepted responsibility. I wanted him to tell me I was right. When I stepped into his dorm, he was already standing there with his head down and looking defeated. Instead of opening my mouth to even say one word, I walked up and gave him a hug.

"Bobby, it's OK." He began to sob, and apologized, and told me he did not know what had happened in the hearing. He was adamant that he had accepted responsibility and that the commissioners just had it for him because he had also disclosed about the pregnancy of his wife.

Before I could even say anything, he then looked up at me with a haunted look and said, "I even told them there was a shadow that had startled me, and they didn't believe me." His eyes had taken on that thousand-yard stare that is so common for men who have done decades in prison, and Bobby was no longer present with me.

At that moment, I knew I would never be able to get through to Bobby. He was the only one who would be able to come to terms with the script he had told himself about the day of the murder. He had told himself a series of lies for so long and believed that it had happened like that. I was in way over my head, and I felt stupid for thinking that I could help someone to go to the board and accept responsibility for something they had lied to themselves about for decades.

Bobby refused to sit down with me ever again. We still interacted on a superficial level, and he still would come by and leave his signature book and cookie on my bed, but we never connected and discussed our respective journeys of personal development ever again. I had lost my friend who had given me such a crucial lesson on personal responsibility. It was sad and discouraging, yet I told myself I had to look into my own lies that I had spun for myself over the years and make sure to eradicate them. Much easier said than done, I was realizing.

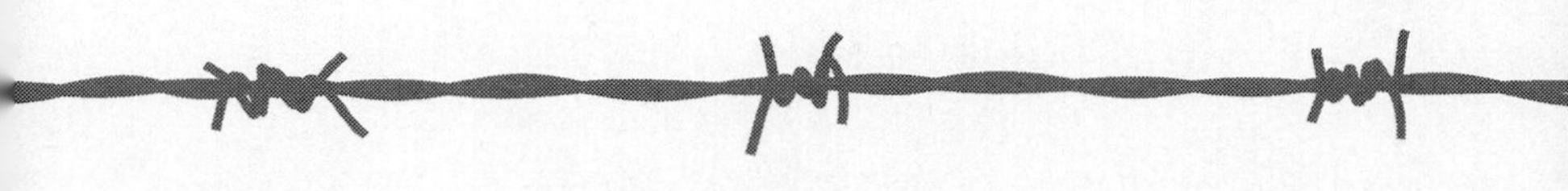

CHAPTER 10

THE JUDGMENT

PRESIDING COMMISSIONER: OK, we're on the record. The time is now 9:03.Today's date is March 7th, 2013We're located at California State Prison, Solano. Today we're here for an Initial Parole Consideration Hearing for Quan Le Huynh. How do you pronounce your last name, sir?

INMATE HUYNH: Huynh, sir.

PRESIDING COMMISSIONER: OK. Your CDCR number, sir, is T-03632 You were received into CDCR on 12/26/2000from Los Angeles County for Murder in the First Degree—correction, Murder in the Second Degree. And you received a term of fi teen years to life with a minimum eligible parole date of 5/24/2014.

INMATE HUYNH: Yes.

PRESIDING COMMISSIONER: OK, sir. We've had the opportunity to review your central file. You will be given the opportunity to correct or clarify the record as we proceed. Nothing that happens here today will change the fin ings of the court. We're not here to retry the case. We're here for the sole purpose of determining your suitability for parole. Do you understand that today?

INMATE HUYNH: Yes, sir, I do.

I sat at a long wooden conference table. Inside the boardroom were two commissioners, a representative from the district attorney's office, and my own attorney. One commissioner was the presiding commissioner, the main one running the hearing, while the other was the deputy commissioner. There was also a correctional officer standing off to the side for security purposes. In front of each of us was a microphone.

The hearing was being recorded and transcribed. This was my Initial Parole Consideration Hearing. Initial Parole Consideration Hearings were conducted one year prior to each prisoner's minimum eligible parole date. Even if I were to be found suitable, the earliest I could go home was at least another year.

During a hearing, the presiding commissioner read into the record the case history and facts of the crime. From reading many transcripts over the years, I knew the presiding commissioner would ask me about my crime. After that, the deputy commissioner would ask questions, then go into post-conviction factors including my accomplishments and my in-prison behavior. Then the representative from the DA's office would ask me clarifying questions through the panel. Typical hearings could last anywhere from three to five hours.

I had visualized this day many times and understood the procedure in and out because of all the transcripts I had read. Still, my heart was thumping in my chest, and my palms were sweating. My nerves were getting the best of me, and my mind was already generating random and rapid thoughts.

A few years ago, I had learned from a meditation book a small hack to help calm myself: anchors to help achieve a meditative state of mind. Most people associated anchors with the breath or mantras, but in this book I learned about physical anchors. During meditation, I began to anchor my feelings of peaceful serenity by squeezing my left wrist. This would create a physical anchor for me to calm down. During meetings or discussions in groups, when I was feeling nervous or frustrated, I could slide my right hand over my left wrist, give myself a gentle squeeze, and a small state of calm would settle over my mind. Nobody ever knew what I was doing, and it helped. Under the table, I squeezed the wrist of my left hand, breathed in through my nose, and felt my heart rate lower. I became present in the room.

Sitting across the conference table from me were the presiding commissioner, an African American male, and the deputy commissioner, a Hispanic woman. The deputy commissioner was observing me in between writing down notes, no kindness on her face. Seated to my left was my attorney; she shuffled some papers and gave me a reassuring wink. I gave her a smile back. At the far end of the conference table on my left was the representative from the district attorney's office. He had sandy blond hair and a slight mustache. He was on his cell phone and looked to be texting out a last message. Although he seemed uninterested, I knew from transcripts that the deputy district attorneys were the most adversarial in the hearings.

Leading up to the hearing, my attorney and I had discussed several ways we could approach it. She was surprised when I first disclosed that I wanted to admit to the shooting but then agreed that would be the best way. She stated most clients wanted to admit to only the bare minimum. But we both knew my admitting to more would add credibility to my testimony. It was also in alignment with how I wanted to live my life. There was a part of me, of course, that was still scared of admitting that I lied at trial. I was unsure how that would come across to the commissioners.

During a typical hearing, the commissioners would gauge if the prisoner was suitable for parole. It was rare for someone to be found suitable. When a prisoner is denied parole, the length of a denial was set for three, five, seven, ten, or fifteen years. A person with multiple write-ups who did not accept any type of responsibility could be denied another hearing for ten or fifteen years. I noticed men who had perfect prison records were typically denied for three or five years but sometimes could also be given seven or ten years, depending on what they said in their hearings. I knew one of the biggest obstacles to overcome for me to minimize a lengthy denial were my prison write-ups and having been deemed a program failure. But I only wanted to tell my truth and share my self-understanding.

The presiding commissioner began to read into the record my procedural and case history, with a deep, booming voice. He began to ask me seemingly innocuous questions, such as where was I born, how many siblings I had, and where my family now lived. I knew that he was asking me in order to provide a baseline for how I reacted to and answered questions when telling the truth. It was a classic interrogation technique, one in which he would lull me into a false sense of security, then throw me a question from left field. But knowing what a person would do and actually experiencing it were two different things. As we discussed my teenage years, he probed and asked, "Why did you join a street gang?"

"I joined a street gang at that time because it gave me a sense of acceptance and belonging with my Vietnamese peers," I answered.

He asked me to further clarify, and I began to share my own struggles with self-identity growing up in Utah. I shared how I never felt like I fit in and then felt like I was also rejected by my Vietnamese peers when our family had first moved to California. After my father's death when I was thirteen, I never developed a healthy self-concept and gravitated toward other kids who felt outcast in society. The commissioner then asked me about my first arrest. Although we were discussing things that had happened over twenty years ago, I knew it was of the utmost importance how I described it today. With my words, the commissioners would be able to get a feel for how I saw the world. If I continued to use the language of blame or not accept responsibility, or if I tried to minimize my culpability in some way, those words would then be used as evidence to deny me parole. I had seen it in enough transcripts to realize that harmless questions were sometimes the most dangerous.

We then discussed my case history of previous arrests and convictions. He confirmed the dates of each of my arrests, institutions I was housed at, and we got into a rhythm. I continued to answer yes to each statement. Suddenly he stopped, looked up at me, and said, "What happened to Mr. Nguyen?" His voice echoed off the walls.

The way he asked it caught me by surprise; he had settled my nerves with his statements, then went after me and asked about my victim. I noticed the deputy commissioner had stopped scribbling notes and was listening to what I would say next. I knew what I would have to do, but I was still scared. It would be the first time I had ever admitted on the record that I was the shooter. I reached under the table and squeezed my wrist again for reassurance.

"I shot and murdered him."

I shared how I followed the victims for over twenty miles and coordinated the ambush for the murder. From the corner of my eye, I noticed the representative from the district attorney's office writing furiously in his notepad. I could tell that everyone in the room was absolutely surprised by what I was admitting to.

Most prisoners would never admit to the bare minimum, and here I was giving them much more than I had been found guilty of. I felt this was not only necessary for the record but also for the continued cleansing of my soul. I answered every question that was thrown at me, although I noticed time and again my own tendency to want to minimize my culpability. I was mindful to not use any words that could be construed that I was not accepting responsibility. I fought the urge to preface every answer with the words "but," "just," or "only." My palms were sweaty, and I rubbed them across my thighs. It was terrifying answering the questions. After what seemed like an eternity, the presiding commissioner relented and changed directions. He started reading into the record support letters from friends and family. I began to breathe.

The hearing was then passed over to the deputy commissioner. This was the part of the hearing that would review my post-conviction factors. She began to read into the record trade classes and certifications that I had completed.

My mind started running again. Did we already finish the first part of the hearing? Fuck! I'm not sure if I communicated everything to the best of my ability. I wish there was more time to share how I see the world! I squeezed my wrist again to center myself as the deputy commissioner continued to confirm each of my accomplishments. She got me answering questions in a smooth rhythm and then stopped.

"OK. The proverbial elephant in the room here really is the 115s." She was referring to my prison write-ups. I felt both confused and elated. *The proverbial elephant should be my admitting that I lied on the stand and got away with first-degree murder! Not my prison write-ups!* But what she said affirmed to me that I had done right by admitting to everything. I sat up straight in my chair and leaned forward.

She asked about my thought process behind each of my prison write-ups. It was similar to how the presiding commissioner had asked about each of my arrests. *She's trying to see how I describe my culpability!* My internal alarms went off, and I now knew this hearing was far from over. It was important how I answered these questions also. If not, the commissioners could use my words to support a multiyear denial at many more hearings to come. I was intentional in what I was saying, and we continued our dance of words.

Every opportunity I had to bash myself, I did, and I realized I was no longer uncomfortable with laying out the worst parts of my character defects. I also noticed, though, that the deputy commissioner was becoming a little frustrated. She was looking for ways to twist my words, but I was not giving her an opportunity through my answers. She finally relaxed and stated on the record that she had no more questions. It took me by surprise, and I saw a triumphant look on her face. There wasn't much time to think as the representative from the district attorney's office took over the questioning.

He began by questioning me again about my statements at trial, how I had lied on the stand, and had gotten away with a special circumstance murder. He began to ask more, but then the presiding commissioner interrupted and stated we were not there to retry the case. The deputy district attorney asked a few last questions about my case and then stated, "I'm done."

My attorney then took over. She asked questions about my self-understanding about the night of the murder. What motivated me, what was my emotional state, and why I was capable of killing another human being. I talked, but I felt quite disconnected. This was a topic I had talked about for the last few years, but it had always been in a safe space. There was support and a mutual search for understanding and empathy in those groups. Inside this boardroom, though, it felt quite adversarial.

I spoke and expounded on my self-understanding. Yet, I did not share from my heart. It did not feel like a space where I could share without judgment. I was mindful enough to not let my own beliefs be the lens with which I was experiencing the whole hearing. I could feel the energy of the commissioners, and it was not pleasant. In the middle of the question-and-answer period with my attorney, it dawned on me how ridiculous this all felt.

What did it all matter how I was able to transform my inner world? What does any of this matter in comparison to the fact that I am here for the murder of another human being? Why are we speaking only about my so-called accomplishments? With those thoughts, we took a quick break and came back for everyone's closing statements.

The deputy district attorney started off by saying I was unsuitable for parole. I had read enough transcripts to not pay too much attention to what he was saying because a lot of it was standard language. He cited case factors, my in-prison disciplinary write-ups, and my criminal history as reasons why I should not be paroled.

Somewhere in his rant, though, his tone changed. It was no longer robotic, but there was feeling and substance behind what he said next. He stated, "My outrage is not a factor in parole, but I want to get it on the record. He ought to be kissing the floor every day that he even has a right to have a parole hearing because by his conduct, which he's admitted here today, this was a gang crime to enhance the status of the gang and his personal role in the gang. It was a drive-by shooting and he was the shooter. His lies to the jury have benefited him."

My head spun, and I realized he was right. I'm supposed to be on death row or serving life without possibility of parole, and yet I have a chance for parole because of my lies.

My attorney, though, would have none of that. She began to highlight why I was suitable for parole. Her arguments sounded empty in comparison to the comments by the deputy district attorney. But as I listened to what she was saying, I realized I was no longer the same person who came into prison fourteen years ago. I had evolved, and my inner world had transformed. She highlighted the fact that I was making a difference in the prison community. When she finished, I was feeling a little more grounded and present. We had had numerous conversations about my inability to forgive myself, and hearing her speak gave me a little reassurance that I had been able to make a change in my life. They then turned it over for me to give my closing statement.

THE CLOSING STATEMENT

"I would like to thank the panel for their patience today and for providing me with an opportunity to speak. I am deeply ashamed and sorry for my actions on January 15th, 1999. I was an arrogant, violent, egotistical gang member that murdered a living, breathing, human being named Minh Nguyen. I permanently altered and shattered numerous lives connected to this young man, and there will never be a way to make it right again, ever. I rejected everything my mother and my faith had instilled in me and instead set down that long, dark path of death and destruction. In the process, I diminished everything in me that was true and right and good, and brought intense evil and pain upon the world.

Today, despite my horrific failures, I believe I have a chance at redemption. Today, I know it is my small, everyday choices that will continue to transform me, over the course of my lifetime, into something worth salvaging. I am no longer afraid of failure, accepting that I am a flawed human being. I know of the evil that I have done and now choose a path of spirituality, love, and discipline. CDCR has given me a prime opportunity for rehabilitation and restoration and I am extremely grateful. I have grown in self-awareness and today have healthy coping skills.

I believe I am ready to be a contributing and law-abiding citizen, and I humbly ask this panel to accept me back into society."

CALIFORNIA BOARD OF PAROLE HEARINGS: DECISION

PRESIDING COMMISSIONER: The time is now 12:25All parties have returned to the room in the matter of Quan Huynh. Huynh was received into CDCR from Los Angeles County for murder. He's serving a sentence of fi teen years to life for Second Degree Murder. He was received into CDCR on December 26th, 2000. Minimum eligible parole date is May 24th, 2014The victim was Minh Nguyen, twenty-six years old at the time of his death. This panel has reviewed all information received from the public and all relevant information that was before us today in concluding that the prisoner is not suitable for parole because he poses a present risk of danger to society or a threat to public safety if released from prison. The fi st consideration which weighs heavily against suitability would be the gravity of the commitment offense. This was a calculated drive-by shooting on the part of Quan Huynh and his crime partners that resulted in the death of the victim. What is the motive for this crime? Well, there are several motives. The fi st motive that is a drive-by gang-related shooting. Mr. Huynh was a member of a street gang when this crime was perpetrated. But Mr. Huynh also said in testimony and various documents that, well, he lost a management position, so he had some anger that was built up inside of him. Furthermore, he was involved in gang-related activities as a member of a street gang prior to this life crime. Other factors the board utilized today in determining his suitability would be the serious misconduct while incarcerated. Mr. Huynh's misconduct while incarcerated was a bit atrocious. Mr. Huynh's disciplinary history resulted in him being classified by the institution as a program failure. They call that C-status. Now, in my time of doing parole hearings, Mr. Huynh is the only one I've seen classified as C-status. I haven't seen anybody classified as C-status. I've seen a lot of people that have a lot of numerous violations, but he's the fi st one I've seen classified as C-status

DEPUTY COMMISSIONER: Just a couple things I want to add to that, Mr. Huynh. Not only did you have the cell phone, but you were also using it to run an underground business. You were trafficking tobacco. You might have been trafficking cell phones as well. I don't know. I don't know what else you were trafficking. And those are additional crimes for which you haven't even been held accountable. It's not just that, but in your case, it's clear and you even stated here that, you know, I was selfish. I was egotistical. You know, I didn't think the rules applied to me. All of that is true. You have a real sense of entitlement. I have to tell you, sitting here across the table from you, you don't have an ounce of humility. You actually come across as someone who is somehow holier than thou. And you may not see that. But we're looking at you from a different perspective. I don't think you've taken a hard look at yourself. You have some very deep-seated character flaws and personality—I guess you could call them flaws, but just part of your personality, part of who you are, of why you choose to lie, why you choose to deceive, why you choose to get away with whatever it is you can get away with, why you can try to come in here and try to pull one over on the panel. Maybe that's still part of your persona. I don't know. It may or may not be.

PRESIDING COMMISSIONER: In terms of your denial length, we looked at the fi teen- and ten-year denial. And by clear and convincing evidence due to your programming and your stable social history and signs of remorse, we determined that you don't need a ten- or fi teen-year denial. We then went to the next category of seven, five, and three years, and we determined by clear and convincing evidence for the same reasons of your positive programming that a fiv -year denial would be appropriate for you. As part of Marsy's Law, you have the right to request the board conduct your next hearing earlier than the denial length we issued here today provided there's been a change of circumstances or new information that establishes a reasonable likelihood you don't need additional time. You do that by use of a BPH 1045AYou can do that anytime, but you can only do it once every three years. And you're a smart guy and you will—I have no doubt that you will—probably be looking into that. So we wish you luck. The time is now 12:5 This hearing is now concluded.

INMATE HUYNH: All right. Thank you.

I was heartbroken, not because of the denial but from the hurtful words that were said to me by the deputy commissioner. Little did I know at the time, I would see her again at my next parole hearing, promoted to a presiding commissioner, and the experience at that hearing would be even worse.

While awaiting an escort in the holding tank, my attorney looked at me through the bars of the mechanical gate. She read my mind. "Quan, I want you to not take to heart what the deputy commissioner said right now. In a denial, they have to go over the top. She was uncomfortable with the candidness of your testimony today. I would have thought she would appreciate it, but obviously she did not."

Of course, her words did not reduce the harshness from my own inner critic. *Am I still that ugly of a person and not even aware of it?* Back on the yard, only a few of my close friends came by to check on me. For the most part, I noticed that a lot of people stayed away. The prison grapevine whispered that anyone I coached for the board was stupid because if I knew what was going on, how did I get a five-year denial? This, despite the fact that over half of the men whom I had helped had been found suitable for parole. I noticed I continued to dwell on the deputy commissioner's words the most. My natural tendency was to bottle feelings of hurt up, yet this time I decided to start talking about them with close friends who would listen and be able to hold the space with me.

That same weekend, we had an AVP workshop, and I was one of the facilitators on the team of three prisoners and two volunteers from the outside. A fellow facilitator, Jay, was the team lead. He looked like a bear of a man, with a big beard and large arms. He had a lazy eye that rolled off to the left, and he looked intimidating, yet was one of the gentlest souls that I knew in the AVP community.

"OK, so each of us are going to say what we would like feedback on this weekend," Jay said. We began to go around. For the most part, everyone was saying they needed feedback on how to present a certain exercise. He then turned to me.

"OK," I began. "Some of you may not know this, but I went to the board last week and was given a five-year denial." The groans around the table felt supportive. "There were some hurtful things that were said inside the boardroom that I would like to share, though. The deputy commissioner told me that I did not have an ounce of humility in my presentation. She said I have a sense of entitlement." Everyone was quiet, and I continued. "What I would like feedback from the team is this: if I say, do, or even act like anything that exudes any type of ego or pridefulness, or lack of humility, I would like your feedback on it. You know, arrogance is one of my biggest issues, and something I will most likely struggle with my whole life. But if you can help me remove some of it in some way, then you are helping me to become a better human being."

The team stayed quiet, and Jay observed me, with his lazy eye drifting to the left again. "I'm not going to tell you that you are not egotistical, Quan, because I know that is not what you are looking for us to say to you. I hope you realize that you can't always beat yourself up, though. But if you do anything like that, me and the team will be sure to let you know."

The workshop went well. The participants were able to explore issues that contributed to violence in their lives. I believed the work we were doing transformed the prison culture at Solano.

But over those three days, there was never any feedback about ego, pride, or lack of humility for me. It would have been easier in my mind if they were able to point something out, then I could fix it. During our team debrief, one of the facilitators lavished praises on Jay and said she had no constructive feedback for him. I found myself getting frustrated because I saw issues where he could have led an exercise better. *Are they all blind, or are they uncomfortable with giving feedback? Maybe they see stuff about me, too, and can't tell me.* I became upset and realized I had crossed my arms. My body was tense. I sat up straight, took a deep breath, and squeezed my left wrist under the table to center myself. I became present with the team and noticed I had judged each of them. The arrogance was still there, right under the surface. This is what the deputy commissioner must have seen!

That night in my journal, I vented. Why was I still struggling with my ego? In what other areas of my life was I still filled with disdain for people? I had condemned Bobby for not taking responsibility and in my mind lynched each of my team members for not being able to point out things to help me address the deputy commissioner's feedback. Why was I so bothered by her words? Why did I have to correct things to gain her approval or look for reasons to prove her wrong? Why could I not sit with her feedback and own my part in it? At the least, I was ineffective with her. I knew she was right; there were parts of me that still exuded arrogance, but I could not figure out how to address it. Journaling helped me to accept that I did not have to fix all my shortcomings overnight.

That began to ease the hurt until I received a letter from my aunt the following week. She was my father's younger sister, and according to my mom, she was my father's favorite. We had been writing letters for the last couple of years, and I admired her wisdom and spirituality. I loved receiving her letters because they were always encouraging and filled with such love and kind words. This letter, though, felt different. She alluded to the fact that the family was concerned for my mental health and well-being. In her words, she wanted me to keep my expectations realistic. She had heard about my five-year denial. Obviously, she had researched and found out only a small percentage of California prisoners were ever paroled from a life sentence. That was the context in which she wrote the letter, I am sure. But with my recent denial and the hurt that I was still feeling, this letter further broke my heart. What did she mean realistic expectations? Did that mean I should resolve myself to the fact that I should die in prison? I realized my own family did not even think I could ever go home. It felt the letter said to basically not put all my eggs in one basket and to live the rest of my days in prison and not try to go home. It also felt like it diminished all the internal work I had done the past couple of years. I had been able to transform the very fabric of my prison life and existence to one of inner peace and joy. At that moment, I felt so alone in my journey. I wrote a letter in response.

May 9, 2013

Dearest Co Hue,

I hope this letter finds you and Uncle Al in the best of health. Things on my end are good. I have recently decided to learn how to play the guitar. It is so relaxing, and I hope to one day play songs for little Alyssa.

To address some of the questions and comments you had in this last letter—I do agree the root cause of my disappointment was my hope to receive a favorable decision from the board. I do understand that chances for parole are slim, but if I never believe in myself, who will? My whole life I have been afraid of failure or anything that casts me in an unfavorable light, and I know of the dark path I chose because of that fear. I knew going into this hearing, if I came back on the prison yard with a big denial, I would be confronted with those same feelings of defeat, humiliation, shame, disappointment…which I was always afraid to face. And that's exactly how I felt when I came back. At Solano, I live in a dorm setting, so everyone knew I was going that day. And because of the path I have chosen to walk, I have my fair share of detractors. Needless to say, many of the men who are still stuck in their ways were gloating when I was denied parole.

The difference for me, though, was I did not hide from those feelings but embraced them for what they were. The denial does not define me, and I am still not afraid to say I am confident that I will one day go home. Don't worry, I am not being delusional.

OK, I will talk to you soon!

Much Love Always, Quan

P.S. My father (your brother) passed away 25 years ago yesterday. I still miss him.

Writing the letter itself was cathartic for me because as the words flowed, I realized my world in prison had been transformed. It was no longer punishment but had become a journey of refinement for my mind and my soul. It did not matter if I was going to die in prison because I was going to live in it free regardless of whatever happened.

CHAPTER 11

MURDERERS AND RAPISTS

DEPUTY COMMISSIONER: All right. So we're going to talk about your post-conviction, sir.

INMATE HUYNH: Yes.

DEPUTY COMMISSIONER: You have a couple vocations you completed, correct? Those are both totally completed, right?

INMATE HUYNH: Yes, they're all—they're both completed.

DEPUTY COMMISSIONER: You're a facilitator in AVP. Victims Awareness, you're an instructor. Personal Transformation, so that's psychotherapy essentially.

INMATE HUYNH: Yes.

During our group therapy sessions, I began to question the way we viewed life in prison, especially when it came to the hierarchical pecking order. Typically, someone incarcerated for a gang-related murder was at the top of the food chain, and at the bottom of it were the rapists and child molesters. That was a badge that I held on to for many years. Every time there were conversations or I met new people, I made sure to somehow allude to my crime and how I was incarcerated because I was snitched on by my own homeboy. It was a way for me to continue to build stature with those around me.

Our psychotherapy group met once a week in a stuffy room around a dark brown table and discussed readings from *The Epictetus Club*, a book that we were all reading together as part of the group process. One day, our therapist brought in a form for the twelve of us to fill out. It was some type of personality test. But when I started answering the questions, I realized the test was for people incarcerated for sex offenses. The other men in the group quickly came to the same conclusion. We all began to look up at each other suspiciously.

One of the participants, John, pushed his test away in disgust. He was white and had faded tattoos that looked like dark splotches up both arms. The only thing I could make out was the silhouette of a swastika on the inside of his elbow. He was one of the quieter men in our group, but whenever he spoke, it was always direct and to the point.

"OK, why are we doing this?" he snarled. "Somebody in this group must be a chester." The energy shifted in the room, and everyone was deathly quiet.

Our psychologist's face turned beet red. "No, I'm so sorry! I gave you guys the wrong form." She gathered up our half-finished tests and shoved them into a manila folder. I noticed she was too flustered to straighten them all out, and the corners were not lined up. For some reason, it bothered me, and I wanted to fix it for her.

Nobody spoke. I noticed everyone had withdrawn, and it took every ounce of my will to slowly unfold my arms from each other. During that time, I was reading quite a few books on mindfulness, and I had been using our therapy group as a testing ground for things I was trying to practice. One of them was being mindful of my breath and how it related to my thoughts. I was breathing quite shallowly. I then began to examine my thoughts. First, I was worried about the guys in the group thinking that I was a child molester. It was irrational, but I saw the same fear in all of the men sitting around the table. Nobody in prison ever wanted to be known as a child molester. I still had nightmares about my first mission of attacking a child molester when I had turned eighteen and how we had stomped on and split open his head.

Our psychologist wrapped up the group, but the tension was still evident. During that week, I saw news accounts regarding Elizabeth Smart, the girl who was abducted, raped, and held captive in Utah. She wrote a book, and in every interview with her on the news, I saw what a beautiful soul she was and how her family was extremely grateful to have her alive. At that time, I was facilitating Victims Awareness classes and was feeling extremely guilty regarding the man I had killed. It bothered me how his mother must still be suffering to this day. I could not stop myself from crying when watching Elizabeth Smart speak. She was such a living testament to the power of forgiveness and healing.

With that turmoil of emotions, I stepped into our therapy group the following week. The guys were still upset from the previous week, and our therapist got right into the discussion. She started off by saying that it was her mistake for giving us an assessment that, although universal, had more context for those who were incarcerated for sex crimes. I noticed the men were still looking around at each other tentatively.

John was still tense. "Bottom line, is anyone in this group a chester? I am not doing a group with any chesters!" He pounded the table for emphasis. Our therapist remained quiet, and we all began to mutter that none of us were child molesters or sexual predators. I nodded my head in agreement but felt quite conflicted inside.

"So let's examine this," she broke her silence. "Why this intense aversion for those that are in for sex crimes?"

This caused quite the discussion. Everyone began to chime in on how rapists were the lowest of the low and that any man who would rape a child or woman was the worst thing in the world. This is what we all believed. This is what was ingrained in me from the first time I stepped into juvenile hall. This was a fundamental part of my belief system. Even in everyone's comments and discussions, I felt the anger rise in me in thinking about those who would do such despicable things to other human beings. Except there was one major problem. In my gut, I felt we were looking at it all wrong.

I felt my heart pounding in my chest, and I became aware of my breath going in, then going out. The voices of everyone began to fade. Although I did not know the exact words they were now saying, I could feel the intensity of what they were talking about. The more I slowed down my thoughts, the more I got a glimpse of how they perceived the world. *We were all wrong!*

I was wrong! I had been wrong all these years of my life. Then another horrible thought crept in. *What else about my life and beliefs was I wrong about? And why is it every time I think I know myself, I discover something new?*

I squeezed my wrist to center myself. "I have something to say." Everyone turned to me. "I think we are looking at this wrong, you guys." John glared across the table at me, and I could feel everyone ready to pounce on my next words. I breathed in and felt my chest rise. "You guys all know I am here for murder. Some of you have been in Victims Awareness with me. And we all say that we feel remorseful for what we have done. Yet, somehow, if we are still holding ourselves above someone else for their crimes, are we not diminishing our victims and their suffering?"

John was staring at me. I looked him in the eye. "John, I have heard you speak about the suffering of the family of your victims. I think you do feel remorseful for your actions." I noticed he sat back a little in his seat. I then looked up at everyone else. "But let me ask you all a question. Has everyone been watching the news accounts of Elizabeth Smart and her ordeals when she was kidnapped and raped repeatedly? Do you guys see how happy her family is to have her still alive?" The men nodded in agreement. "I am only imagining the mother of the man I killed, if she had a choice, would much rather have her son alive today, even if I had kidnapped, raped, and sodomized him. Guys, I am sorry to say this, but murderers are lower than even the rapists."

Most of the men did not say anything, including John. Two men, both in for murder, argued that rapists were still the worst. One of them even said, "Well, everyone knows that." And I realized he is stating a belief that is false but so real in his mind. After our group session was over, the psychologist asked me to stay back for a bit because she had something to discuss with me. After everyone walked out, she turned to me.

"I want to commend you for your courage today in speaking up. That was very brave of you to share your own thoughts. So thank you." She smiled at me.

"Well, that's how I felt, Doctor. I realized as we were discussing this whole thing that we all have been looking at it wrong. These rules that we have about prison and the pecking order are all created in our minds. And some of the guys do not see it! I am starting to think about what other things we are looking at wrong in here."

"Yes! That would be great for you to examine! Let's talk about your thoughts on this at our next one-on-one session." Besides the weekly group therapy sessions, we met about once every other week. She walked with me down the hallway and fumbled with her keys to open the sally port door for me to get back to my yard. The bronze skeleton key finally slid into the lock, and I heard it click open. "Bye, Quan. Have a great rest of your week."

I walked out to my yard and looked around. Everyone was doing what they did every day on the prison yard. At the basketball court, there were two groups playing. On one end were the blacks. At the other end, were the whites and Hispanics. The people watching were also grouped up by race. At the handball courts, it was the same thing: whites and Hispanics playing on one court, blacks on another. I noticed the same thing at the workout stations. Then I looked over the yard, particularly the concrete tables, and how they were also grouped up by race. *This is a world that we have created for ourselves in here, with all these rules and ways of conducting ourselves, and none of us know that we are all wrong.* As I watched, I realized there had been plenty of other prisoners who had walked this path long before me. I did not recognize or hear them at the time. In my arrogance, I dismissed them as idiots or cowards who had not conformed to prison politics. *I'm barely just starting on this journey.* I felt excited about what else I could discover.

The soft crunch of someone walking up nearby on gravel got my attention. I always had to be aware of what was going on around me. As I turned, I tensed up my body because I thought someone was coming up to stab me. Perhaps I said too much in our group today, and word had already got out that I was defending rapists. I had the fleeting thought, *Maybe this is another belief that is false.* I looked up and it was John.

"Hi, John." Nearby, a discarded plastic wrapper from our lunch cookies scratched its way across the asphalt from a slight breeze.

"Hey, I wanted to talk to you about what you said today." He stopped and turned sideways and looked off into the distance. He crossed his arms, and his hands covered his faded swastika. "You gave me a lot to think about, so I wanted to thank you. Most of the guys in there would never admit it. But I think you are right." He turned to me and shook my hand. We briefly made eye contact, and I saw the tears in his eyes. He let go, put the palm of his hand over his face and quickly wiped away any trace of tears. With that, he turned around and walked off.

I watched as he strolled up the pavement toward the concrete table where some of the old-timer whites would be. Most of these guys had been affiliated with biker gangs, skinhead groups, or a racially divisive gang in prison at one time or another, all of them with faded tattoos, symbols of hate and death splotched across their necks, chests, and arms. Each of these men, I am sure, had some time or another done some extremely violent and evil things. But all I saw were lost and confused souls that perhaps had not yet awakened.

CHAPTER 12

CONVERSATIONS WITH MY MOTHER

PRESIDING COMMISSIONER: You were convicted by jury November 3rd, 2000.

INMATE HUYNH: Yes.

PRESIDING COMMISSIONER: For 187Murder in the Second Degree, being found not guilty of remaining counts with special allegations found not to be true. The victim was Minh Nguyen, for the transcriber, fi st name spelled M-I-N-H, last name spelled N-G-U-Y-E-N. What happened to Nguyen?

INMATE HUYNH: I'm sorry?

PRESIDING COMMISSIONER: What happened to Mr. Nguyen?

INMATE HUYNH: I shot and murdered him.

PRESIDING COMMISSIONER: Why did this happen?

INMATE HUYNH: I had come out the club that night at the Arena Nightclub. When I came out, I had found out that some of my homeboys had gotten into a fight with a g oup of guys from a different gang.

I had a great bunky named Ralphie. We got along from day one when I first met him, and I admired his spirit and simple love of life. He also began to teach me how to play the guitar, and we had bunked up about a year after my first board hearing. He and I would have many different conversations with each other about family, friends, and our hopes and dreams for the future. Of course, both of our conversations revolved quite a bit around our mothers and the bizarre family dynamics each of us had experienced growing up. Ralphie was in prison for killing another man in his backyard. His friend was getting choked out, so Ralphie had jumped in, slammed his face into the ground, then bludgeoned him to death with a pickax. He covered up the body in the backyard and dumped it the next day. His crime was brutal and cold-blooded, yet he was the gentlest soul on the yard.

One day, while we were cooking dinner, I was talking to him about how my mom had never told us she loved us. Ralphie was slicing up the sausages with the top of a tuna can that we had sharpened. I was grilling the onions and garlic powder inside an empty tomato can that we had procured from the prison kitchen, over an electric coil that Ralphie and I had removed from one of our hotpots that we used to boil water. "I mean, I know she does and all," I was saying, "but she never says it. She expresses it through her cooking, though, homie. And that woman can cook!" I squirted in a little soy sauce, and the smell of caramelized onions and garlic filled our dorm room.

"Do you love your mom, Quan?" Ralphie asked in his discerning way. He had finished chopping, and the sausage slices were in a neat little pile.

"Of course I do." I removed the onions, added a little water to the tomato can and stirred in some hoisin sauce that we bought from our quarterly packages. I began adding in the sausages so they could stew with the base I had created and would add the onions back in after everything was done. I looked up to see what Ralphie would say next. He always had a way of challenging my thought process.

He was staring at me. "So why don't you tell her? I mean why does she have to tell you first? We both know that our parents were not perfect, and it is on us to take what we like and change the legacy of what we don't, right?" He had a mischievous look on his face. "In fact, I challenge you to tell your mom you love her this Sunday, friendo!" Ralphie began giggling.

Ralphie knew that every Sunday morning, I would get on the wall phone and call home for the allotted fifteen minutes. He also knew that it would be difficult for me to tell my mom that I loved her. "OK, I can do that." I gulped. This was a challenge I knew was worth taking on, no matter how uncomfortable.

After the light had started to come on for me, I made it a habit of calling home on Sunday mornings and listen to my mom. During my earlier years in prison, I would call home, and my mother would tell me about challenges and difficulties in her life. I always felt that I had to fix her problems. Because I could not and felt helpless about it, I would lash out and yell at her and tell her she needed to look at it this way or approach the issue from that way. I never once acknowledged that she had any issues, or if she did, they were all created in her head.

Somewhere along the way, I learned that listening, true active listening, is both an art and a gift. There was something powerful in being there for my mom or any other human being who was suffering in some way. One of the other great gifts was the realization that I did not even have to agree with the person. What they were expressing was only their belief. This gave me a sense of self-awareness in my conversations, and I could remain detached and yet present with each person. I could continue to send good energy toward them.

Sunday came, and as I walked toward the phone that morning, Ralphie peeked over the top of the book he was reading, *The Alchemist*. "Hey, buddy! Make sure you tell your mom I love her, too!" He winked at me and began reading again. No matter how nonchalant his tone, I knew Ralphie would be waiting for me at the bunk area to see if I had followed through on my words. I walked down the stairs from my dorm to the phone sitting on the wall. Nearby, a couple of guys were already warming up for their exercise routines, jogging in place while stretching to prepare their bodies for their burpees and push-ups. At one of the metal tables, a couple of others were setting up to play chess. I looked over the dayroom and saw some men lined up at the hot water spigot, most of them pouring hot water into their cups of instant coffee. The dayroom porters were already sweeping and mopping up the floors. Another group had closed off one of the restroom areas to begin cleaning the toilets and sinks. The distinct hollow flushing of the institutional toilets added to the noise of another day about to begin in prison. I could smell the overpowering stench of the Pine-Sol that was used to clean the whole building.

We had sign-ups for fifteen-minute phone calls, and Sunday mornings were the busiest. There was a man still on the phone that I had signed up for. We made eye contact, and he nodded and held up one finger to let me know he would be getting off shortly. "OK, darling," he spoke into the phone. He was seated on the metal seats that were under every phone and stood up as he turned his back to me. "It is another man's phone time. I will see you and the kids next week." He paused and listened, and then turned toward me. "Yes, OK. I love you, too." He hung up the phone, grabbed it back up, and used a handkerchief to wipe the receiver down, then looked up at me and gave me a wink. "Here you go, folks."

I grabbed the phone with my own paper towel and took out a small spray bottle of disinfectant and sprayed the phone, dial pad, and seat. I always questioned if doing all these things helped to prevent me from getting sick or not, but it made me feel safer, so I continued to do it. I dialed my mom's number and waited while the machine went through the prerecorded messages. The phone pinged, signaling me to state my name, and I said, "Your son." This was my weekly routine of calling my mother on a Sunday morning, but this morning I felt more nervous than ever. I loved my mom more than anything, but there was not any conversation where we ever said the words, "I love you." It felt unnatural to me. The dial tone on my end pinged again, and I heard her pick up.

The robotic message stated, "You have a collect call from…your son"—it paused and then continued—"an inmate at the California State Prison at Solano. If you accept, dial five now." The long beep was interrupted once I assumed my mother had pressed five on the other end. "Thank you for using Global Tel Link." The voice faded and I heard a slight silence.

"Hello, *Con*," I heard my mom on the other end. *Con* was Vietnamese for child, and it sounded so tender.

"Hi, Mom, how was your week?" This was how our conversations went every Sunday, with me asking how her week went and her updating me with whatever was going on in her life. She was telling me about work and then began telling me about my little niece and how cute she was. Many times, like today, I was amused at what she saw as important, and affirmed whatever she was talking about. Every five minutes or so, our call would be interrupted with the robotic voice reminding us that "this call is monitored and recorded, and from an inmate at a California State Prison." My mother continued after the recording stopped, and I realized after all these years in prison, I would one day like to just have a conversation that was not interrupted or timed in any way. I was not even sure exactly what she was talking about this morning, but I was intentional about being present with her. She continued talking, then the voice interrupted again: "You have sixty seconds."

"Hmm," she sighed. "I like talking to you, *Con*."

"Me, too, Mom." *Does she not realize that I did not even talk for the whole fourteen minutes?* "Anything else going on?" I was stalling, and I could feel my heart pounding in my chest. I knew the operator would interrupt again with a final thirty-second warning.

"No, that's it, *Con*." She was silent. The seconds ticked by, and part of me was hoping that she had hung up prematurely. I stood up from my seat and could feel the sweat on my palms.

"You have thirty seconds," the robotic message reminded us.

I knew it was now or never and knew Ralphie would be waiting on me at our bunk area to see what happened. I gripped the phone. "OK, Mom, you have a good week, OK?"

"Yes, *Con*."

I braced my left hand on the wall and nervously sputtered, "I love you." I heard the intake of her breath on the other end, and before she could respond, I hung up the phone.

My heart was still pounding as I walked up the stairs to my dorm. Halfway up, I saw Ralphie sitting on the top bunk, watching me with a gleam in his eye. "So how goes it, friendo?" he asked.

"It went well," I answered.

"What do you mean, 'It went well'?" Ralphie sat up and then hopped off the top bunk. "Did you tell your mom you love her, and what did she say? You ain't getting off the hook that easy, dude!"

"Well, I did tell her. She was talking the whole time, and then when time ran out, I told her I love her at the end."

Ralphie leaned his head back and was grinning with the biggest smile. "Well, what did she say? Did she say, 'I love you, too'?"

"Um, I don't know. I hung up right after I said it."

"What? Are you kidding me?" Ralphie began jumping up and down in one place while we both laughed. "You know what?" He looked at me with a genuine smile on his face. He opened up his arms and gave me a hug. "I am proud of you, friendo. This is a good beginning. Now it falls on you to tell your mom you love her every week. Next time, make sure to give her a chance to tell you she loves you, too."

We both wiped the tears from our eyes in case the men in our dorm saw us. I knew the tears were healing, but there was a part of me that felt it was still wrong to cry as a man. I was grateful for such a great friendship. Who would have thought that it would take a life sentence for me to figure out what friendship and male bonding was all about. Here was a man that I could share my hopes and dreams with and be completely vulnerable without fear of judgment and scorn. He was also one of many men that I now felt completely connected with. We had both gone to prison for murder but now wanted to lead lives of peace and nonviolence.

The following week, I allowed my mom the space to tell me she loved me, too. It felt unnatural at first, but as time went on, it became a habit. It felt so good to hear that she loved me. Of course, not all our conversations had me feeling good inside.

After I had been denied by the board, I reread my transcripts, particularly where the commissioners stated their reasons for denying me parole. I read books and attended classes that I felt would address each of their reasons for the denial. I filed my petition to advance my hearing after fourteen months. The presiding commissioner had stated on the record that I should submit paperwork if my circumstances had changed. I was unsure what would qualify under those parameters, but I stated in my petition that I felt my circumstances had changed because I had addressed each of their concerns. The common belief among the other prisoners was someone should at least wait close to three years before they file a petition to advance a hearing. I felt it was my time to file mine, though.

Two months after I filed the petition, it was granted. Everyone on the yard said I was going back way too early and I would be denied again. It would take about four months to get my hearing put on the calendar, and I began to prepare myself mentally and emotionally. During this time, my mother came to visit me. Every time I had a visit with my family and friends, I was truly excited and happy inside. This day was no different.

We were sitting inside the visiting room, across from each other at tables that were about a foot high. I never understood why they were so short, but I guess it was to prevent the passing of contraband between visitors and prisoners. She warmed up some cheeseburgers from the vending machines, and I ate them all, even though the bread was a little soggy, some parts warmer than others. Our discussion eventually came around to my upcoming hearing.

"I am so scared about your board hearing, *Con*," she said to me softly. She sat still and looked distraught.

"Mom, what are you scared of?" In a weird way, I found it amusing the way she had undying love for me and my circumstances. She always had a simplistic way of looking at things.

"I am scared for you inside the hearing. I have been praying and praying for you each week at Mass. I even prayed and let God know that I would be willing to die early as long as they let you go home. I am scared that they won't let you go home." She went on and on.

I gently pushed away the urge to laugh or, even worse, lash out at her and dismiss her feelings. Why was she focused on me being at home? *These are her feelings. This is how she sees the world*, I reminded myself. But I also knew there were some things that I felt strongly about, and it was time she understood my position on them. A few years earlier, before my first hearing, I admitted to her I was the shooter and had lied at trial. I apologized to her and let her know I was absolutely sorry for my actions. The way she responded, my gut told me she had known the whole time, yet she had never wavered in her love for me throughout the years. But she never spoke about it again, and it never came up in our conversations.

"Mom, one of two things will happen inside that hearing. Either they find me suitable and they let me go home, or they deny me parole and tell me to come back in a few years." *I wish you could see the way I see it*, I thought to myself.

"But I want you to come home, *Con*. I don't know how much longer I can do this. You have done enough time already. You have done so many good things in here." Her words twisted inside me; she was suffering for things I had done over fifteen years ago. Yet, I still needed her to see and understand the place where I was coming from.

I reached across and held her hands. The familiar dryness of the skin on her palms gave me reassurance. I turned her hands over and looked at them. She still wore the wedding ring from my father, and the thought crossed my mind, *I have never even seen her talk to another man after my father passed away. This is such a precious woman, and I must try to honor her in every way for the rest of my life.* I took a deep breath, looked up at her, and began. "Mom, you do realize what I am in prison for, right?"

She flinched and looked away from me. Her hands squeezed mine weakly, almost as if she did not want to hear what I had to say next. "Mom, don't get me wrong. I want to go home, too. I want you to realize how I see things today. Let me ask you this." I leaned forward in my chair and saw the tears began to well up in her eyes, and she looked away. "Let's say that night I had been the one that had been killed. How would you feel? What if you were to go to the board hearing of the man that had killed me, and he tells you that he is sorry and look at all the good things he is doing in prison now? Do you think that would be enough, Mom? Would that be enough to make up for the child that you had brought into this world?" My words were hurting her, I could tell. She was whimpering and shaking her head no, but I felt it was necessary to continue.

"Mom, the man I killed was named Minh Nguyen. He also has a mother; her name is Julie Nguyen. Where do you think she goes right now if she wants to see her son? A gravestone, like when we want to see Dad, right? Can we just be grateful that I am alive, and that I have become a better person, and that we can still hug each other and be in each other's presence?"

My mother, through her sobs, nodded her head, and I saw that she finally began to understand.

CHAPTER 13

AMAZING GRACE

PRESIDING COMMISSIONER: All right. Mr. Huynh, is there anything that you would like to add, sir?

INMATE HUYNH: Yes. I want to thank you guys both for your time. You know, something was said earlier about my—that I have to rise to the top or to be the leader or—and it was the same thing as my crime. The position of leadership here is about serving the community. It's a position of responsibility and trust. It's not about accolades and showing everybody. It's because in—

PRESIDING COMMISSIONER: Sir, your closing statement.

INMATE HUYNH: OK. So my closing statement. On January 15th, 1999, I shot and killed Mr. Minh Nguyen, tried to shoot and kill his three friends...

The mechanical gate closed in front of me as I stepped into the cell. My attorney stood on the other side of the bars, and she looked at me. "Quan, they are going to deny you parole today. They already had their minds made up before the hearing started, and now they are finding everything they can to justify it. It's not fair! I hate that bitch!" She was referring to the commissioner who had denied me at my previous hearing and had said all the hurtful things about my ego and lack of humility.

I sat down wearily on the wooden slab that protruded from the concrete wall. She was right. We had been in the hearing for about three hours already. I was tired and felt battered all over. The presiding commissioner and the district attorney's representative had been quite vicious in the boardroom.

My attorney had requested a bathroom break, her second one of the day. She had told me during strategy sessions before the hearing that she would request breaks if things were going badly. This would give us time to regroup and give space to what was happening inside the boardroom. The hearing had gone south quick, and I knew I was going to be denied parole again. It was only a matter of how many years they were going to deny me. Inside the hearings, the commissioners could deny a prisoner anywhere from three to fifteen years. I read enough transcripts already to know they were giving me either a three- or five-year denial. My gut felt it would be another five-year denial, but I was hoping it would be only a three-year.

My attorney's face was flush with anger. "OK, I'm not feeling good, and we are not going back in there. This is what we are going to do." She leaned closer to the bars between us and motioned me over. I stood up and walked to her. She leaned forward and whispered, "I am going to say that I am feeling really sick and cannot continue. If I cannot continue, they will have to postpone your hearing for another calendar date. We will probably get put back on the calendar in about three to six months. But they would have to conduct a brand-new hearing, and chances are, you will not have this same commissioner. She doesn't like you, and any other commissioner would have given you a fair hearing. I think you have a good chance to get a parole date at your next hearing. I am not feeling good inside, and that is what we are going to do when we go back in." She shuffled the folder and pen she was holding, like a sword and shield ready to do battle, looked at me, and pursed her lips. "Two can play at this game."

My attorney was right. From the beginning of the hearing, the presiding commissioner was already aggressive in her words to me. Her tone was harsh and sarcastic, and her face shot daggers at me whenever I spoke. Her questions continued to allude to my lack of humility and connection to humanity. At one point in the hearing, when I was sharing about my own process of transformation, she interrupted and told me I sounded like a robot. She said I needed to stop talking. Up to that point, I prided myself on my principles of effective communication. I felt I dealt well with conflict and difficult conversations. But everything I had practiced up to that point did not seem to be working. It felt like she kept bashing me with her words to see how I would react. My mind was reeling from the verbal onslaught, and the words I said in response were not landing well at all. I was mindful to not justify in any way any of my actions regarding my crime or any of the disciplinary write-ups I had received in prison. But I could tell the woman despised me, and there was no way of connecting with her. After the first thirty minutes, I had resolved myself to the fact that she was denying me parole again. I knew the hearing was going to become a matter of record for my future hearings, though, so I made sure to still try to answer her as clearly as possible. She was going above and beyond to deny me, and it felt unfair. We were doing a battle of words in the hearing, and no matter how I tried to connect with her, she was not listening.

My attorney saying she was too ill to continue was my way out, yet I felt conflicted in my gut. If I made this choice—and that is what it was, my choice—it would go against everything I had laid out for myself these last few years. It would go against setting my intention that morning when I read *Your Inner Jewel* to myself. It would go against honoring my victims. It would go against everything I believed in: staying true to my path and my journey. Then I had another thought: denying me parole would give me at least several more years to continue to refine myself. Part of me wanted to look for ways to continue to grow and make an impact on the yard and at this prison. My life was not awful, and although I was not content with where I was at, I was finally at peace with myself and the world. It would not be that bad if I was denied. I realized that.

I looked at my attorney. "No. Let's go back in there. Let's get it over with."

She looked at me like I was crazy. "You do realize they are going to deny you parole today, right?"

I nodded. "Yes, I know. It's OK. This is something that needs to be done. I was here today to hold myself accountable, not to be found suitable."

She shuffled her feet and shook her head at me. "OK. How are you staying so calm in all this? You stayed so calm throughout the hearing, and I couldn't do anything to help you except call these bathroom breaks! You talked about a prayer you do that keeps you grounded. Do you have one to calm us down right now?"

I could tell she was asking only for my benefit, but I wanted to share regardless. "I have a prayer that keeps me calm throughout the day. I chant it as a mantra when things seem to be going wrong, and gives me a sense of peace." I looked at her through the bars. "The prayer was written by Saint Augustine, and I recite it to myself several times throughout the day." I stepped back and closed my eyes and felt my heart still pounding in my chest.

I took a deep, cleansing breath and slowly recited:

> "Breathe in me, Holy Spirit, that my thoughts may all be holy.
>
> Move in me, Holy Spirit, that my work, too, may be holy.
>
> Attract my heart, Holy Spirit, that I only love what is holy.
>
> Strengthen me, Holy Spirit, that I may defend all that is holy.
>
> Protect me, Holy Spirit, that I may always be holy."

I finished the prayer and opened my eyes. There was a deep sense of calm that had once again settled over me. My attorney was looking at me with a polite smile on her face, the kind of smile that says, "You are crazy. I feel so sad for you, but I am not going to say anything."

She instead turned and motioned for the guard inside the booth to open the mechanical doors for me. The gate rumbled on the chains and the door slid open. One of the correctional officers walked out, had me face the wall as he frisked my body from head to toe to make sure I had no weapons, then escorted me back into the boardroom.

They started the tape recorder, and I sat down and began reading my closing statement.

THE CLOSING STATEMENT

"On January 15, 1999, I shot and killed Mr. Minh Nguyen and tried to shoot and kill his three friends—David Tran, Vincent Vivongthanakul, and Andrew Vivongthanakul. When I killed Mr. Minh Nguyen, I did not harm only one human being.

In the immediate aftermath of the shooting, his three friends had to witness him choking to death because the bullets that I shot punctured his lungs. They may have blamed themselves for his death and felt a roller coaster of emotions, ranging from guilt and anger to hurt and fear, and everything else in between. Their view of the world and their place in it was permanently altered. But these are only words on what I imagine the impact my actions have had on each of them; I know full well that I am at best only scratching the surface of how much pain I have caused.

Mr. Minh Nguyen also had a mother named Julie Nguyen. She was never at my trial or any of my board hearings, so she has never had a voice in all this. This is a woman, though, that I am sure suffered in so many countless ways. Once again, I can only imagine. It's hard to picture the horror, shock, and pain she felt in having to identify her son's lifeless body. I do not recall hearing anything about Mr. Minh Nguyen having any siblings at trial, so perhaps I murdered Mrs. Julie Nguyen's only child. There was never any mention of a father, so her son's death has left her utterly alone. She came to the United States with what I am sure were dreams of a better life and being cared for in her golden years by her son. No wedding or birthdays to celebrate, no grandchildren to spoil, no Mother's Day to be honored. I shattered those dreams and any others she may have had for her son. In my culture, one of the first questions strangers ask each other is about family—how many children do you have, what are their occupations, etc. She may have felt shame and stigmatized in some way from friends and family when they whispered that her son was killed by a gang member, with the insinuation that he was also one. Mrs. Julie Nguyen must have been reminded about her son's death a million times since that awful day. Today, she might be filled with guilt for not wanting to share her son's death because nobody can understand her pain. Spiritually, she may question God, the goodness in humanity, and may not even value the worth of living a good life. I also remember during my sentencing she had asked for restitution of $10,000 in funeral costs. The judge had denied it, stating that funeral costs would be set at $5,000. How awful would it be for a mother to have to hear that her burden of missed work days, sick days, and a million other tangible and intangible costs associated with her child's murder was only worth $5,000?

I have also victimized my own family. My mother has had to live with a stigma of her own: to be the mother of a murderer. To this day, she tells her friends that I live far away. I know she blames herself for my situation, like somehow she failed in raising me properly.

For years, I shut out any thoughts regarding my life crime. I am ashamed to say that when I first came into the prison system, I had no sense of remorse. At the time, I could not even grasp the finality of what I had done and the enormity of the pain that I would cause to countless others. In my mind, I justified the whole shooting as something that was gang related; somehow, that made these young men that I tried to kill less human. That cowardly way of not taking responsibility prevented me from making any type of meaningful amends or contributing anything of value to this world. Over these last few years, though, I have started to comprehend, to my disgust, how far reaching my actions on that night were, and am finally living, what I believe, to be a life of atonement and penance that I hope in some small way can give a voice to the pain of Mrs. Julie Nguyen.

I am grateful that I have a chance for parole today. I say that knowing there was nothing particularly mitigating about my case. District Attorney Morrison stated it best at my last hearing: the only reason I have a chance at parole is because I lied at trial and have benefited from it. How do I reconcile that? How do I reconcile that I became a better person at the expense of another human being's life? I have found solace and hope in my faith, with the principles of redemption, and with the understanding that even I am worth salvaging.

I have finally taken advantage of the opportunities that were there for me all along. I am not the same person, thanks to the psychotherapy groups, Alternatives to Violence workshops, self-help, and twelve-step programs I have attended. I have finally addressed what made it capable for me to murder another human being in cold blood; I have explored and changed the unhealthy thought processes that shaped my character and personality flaws. I have transformed the very fabric of my thoughts, my values, and have found purpose and meaning for my life despite my failures as a human being. Today, I live a life of nonviolence. Nonviolence, to me, encompasses the words I use, how I communicate, how I view others, how I view myself, and how I would like to leave an imprint of love and peace on the world. Today, I no longer fear failure, imperfection, setbacks, and difficulties. I have found fulfillment and personal enrichment in connecting with other human beings. I am no longer angry, alone, isolated, and plagued by feelings of self-doubt and worthlessness.

Recently, I spoke to my mother, and she was anxious and concerned about today's hearing, but I felt the need to express to her how I saw things today. It was an extremely difficult conversation, but I posed to her the following scenario.

What if sixteen-odd years ago some gang members murdered me? Now here it is, 2015, and she has an opportunity to be at the board hearing to see the man that had killed me. And that man tells her he is sorry, he has turned his life around. He facilitates workshops and has numerous chronos and certificates; he is not the same person that murdered me. He believes he has addressed the issues that made it capable for him to be a murderer. And I simply asked her, 'Mom, would that make up for the child you brought into this world?' Of course she cried and said no. That's when I told her we should instead be grateful I am alive, she can hug and kiss me, and see me become a better person.

Mrs. Julie Nguyen, on the other hand, will have to go to the cemetery and touch a cold gravestone if she wanted to visit her son. How unfair is that? How bittersweet it will be when the day that I am accepted back into society my family will be celebrating, and there will be an unheard voice still mourning the death of her son.

Mrs. Julie Nguyen is one of my many silent victims I would like to give voice to, no matter where my life leads from here."

CHAPTER 14

LIFE AFTER DEATH

CALIFORNIA BOARD OF PAROLE HEARINGS: DECISION

PRESIDING COMMISSIONER: All right.

DEPUTY COMMISSIONER: Ready?

PRESIDING COMMISSIONER: We are.

DEPUTY COMMISSIONER: Back on the record.

PRESIDING COMMISSIONER: All right. It's about 3:22 and we've reconvened the hearing for the panel's decision in the matter of Mr. Quan Huynh, and the last name is spelled H-U-Y-N-H. All parties are back in the room. Mr. Huynh was received by CDCR December 26, 2000, from the county of Los Angeles. He's serving a sentence of fi teen years to life in the murder of twenty-six-year-old Minh Nguyen. We did consider the testimony presented by Mr. Huynh. Inmate counsel offered her support. The DA remains opposed at this time to a fin ing of suitability. And we had no victim's next-of-kin present today. And the fundamental question we have to answer is whether or not the inmate would pose a potential threat to public safety upon his release. And our decision has to be based on evidence in the record of his current dangerousness. That is the legal standard that we applied in making our decision today. And with that standard in mind, we find that Mr. Huynh does not pose an unreasonable risk of danger to society or threat to public safety and is, therefore, now suitable for parole. Now, Mr. Huynh, this was not an easy decision for us. We debated for a long time arriving at the decision because we were torn about a few matters, but all in all, on balance, we found that there was sufficient information to deem you as someone who is now suitable for parole. The decision that we made does not diminish the fact that the crime that you committed was vicious. It was cruel. It was reckless, disturbing in many ways. You showed absolutely no regard for human life or human suffering. There was one victim who lost his life in the crime, another who was seriously injured. And we were very troubled by your statements today that—where you admitted that your intent was to kill every occupant in that vehicle. You were in a position of leadership. There were multiple victims. These are all reasons to aggravate the term. And the reasons for committing the crime absolutely could not justify your actions in any way, shape, or form. Essentially, you told us that you were angry because you hadn't gotten a management promotion. You were angry about that, so you went to go drink at a bar and there had been this altercation. However, the California Supreme Court has ruled that after a long period of time immutable factors such as the commitment offense may no longer indicate that you are a current risk of danger when there's been a lengthy period of rehabilitation. Ultimately, we felt that there was sufficient information to suggest that you do not pose a threat to public safety. So in your case, sixteen years have passed and many of the circumstances that tend to show suitability are present. You also have accepted full responsibility for your crime and that was evident today not only in your testimony but also in your writings, and we read a lot of your writings prior to the hearing.

My attorney and I could not stop smiling at each other as the commissioners stated their findings for the record. They continued to speak, but their voices seemed to fade away. They finally finished what they had to say, turned off the recorder, and we were off the record. I stood up to shake the presiding commissioner's hand and to thank her. She looked at me and asked, "Have you ever once thought the reason why Gallup turned you down for the management position was not because you were not a fit, but because you were already a convicted felon?" The question threw me for a loop because even after all the internal work I had done, that had never once crossed my mind. Her question made me realize I still had residual feelings of worthlessness that I needed to address.

Journal entry dated June 16, 2015, 11:57 p.m.

Three minutes to midnight. I was found suitable last Friday, June 12. I am still in shock about the whole thing. I am unsure how to feel about it all. I do know that I feel so blessed. So many people have asked me if I am stressed out, or if this is the longest 150 days of my life. Actually for me, today I was thinking, more than ever, to enjoy these last present moments. I have some great and positive relationships in my life, many of whom I will never see again. And so I want to be as present as possible with whoever I come across.

Then I would like to carry that mindset to the streets. Be present with all my loved ones. I want to make sure I am different, not because I murdered someone and got out, but because I murdered someone and yet have a chance to live my life in society again. There are so many goals I would like to achieve, and I am proud to say many of them are simple, such as prayer time. I must continue with my walk of nonviolence.

God has made a way for me, despite my failures as a human being, to do his work. Like St. Francis of Assisi's prayer, he is now making me an instrument of his peace. So I vow to continue looking for ways to do it for him. I have five months to do God's work here. I want to be able to do whatever opens up for me. How else can I inspire hope in the men around me? How else can I share the spark of light that has been ignited in my soul?

I am so grateful to those around me that believed and trusted in me, and saw the best in me, even when I gave them no reason to. And now here it is, five-odd years later, and I must admit there has been a transformation in the way I see the world, my relationships with everyone around me, and my view of my place in it.

To go back to the analogy of the flowers blooming in my wake, what seeds can I still plant before I leave this all behind? I surely cannot wait for this upcoming Training for Facilitators workshop. What an honor it is to be leading the workshop, and helping to contribute to the continued peace in this world.

The next 150 days were challenging for me. I would never see many of these men ever again, I knew that. I had made such meaningful friendships over these last few years. I realized being released would also be a form of loss for me. I had 150 days to grieve the loss of my friends that I would be leaving behind, perhaps forever.

One of the friendships that I knew in particular would hurt me to leave behind was a father figure of sorts, Robert. He was a former Navy corpsman and had been involved in the Vietnam War. In conversations with him, he disclosed he had a Vietnamese wife who had been killed by the Viet Cong. He referred to me as the son he never had. He was tall and rangy with red hair. He always was so soft spoken, and within a couple minutes of talking to him the first time, I knew I was in the presence of someone who was highly intelligent. His prescription glasses were tinted a dark brown so I could never see his pupils, but there was a deep, yet haunted, soul behind them. Robert was convicted of murdering another Vietnam veteran in San Diego and stuffing his body in the refrigerator. About twenty years into his prison sentence for the first murder, Robert was brought up on a cold case for another murder. There were whispers that Robert was responsible for many other bodies and that he was a serial killer.

We had met at church, and he had become a mentor once I got involved with AVP. In the workshops, I saw a facet of Robert that few were able to witness. He had been facilitating for over fifteen years in the prison system and could only be described as magical in those workshops. He was able to weave, create, and captivate so many participants with how he flowed and held the space for everyone, and sparked the most tangible forms of transformation. I saw hardened prisoners go through our workshops and leave as changed souls because of Robert.

Robert and I would have conversations after workshops that we facilitated together. We debriefed and discussed what worked and what could have been improved. I picked his mind on how he did certain exercises compared to others, and he shared with me all his Jedi secrets, as we called them. I referred to him as Obi Wan Kenobi, and he called me his young Padawan. Under his tutelage, I became a capable facilitator. About a year before my second hearing, he was diagnosed with early stage Alzheimer's.

This gentle man was a gift to our community. He helped prisoners pass their GED tests. He helped illiterate inmates write letters to family members. Often, he simply listened to another man's problems. One of the first things I told him when I was found suitable was that I wanted to sit with him for an hour each evening for the next 150 days to hear his story. He had never disclosed much to me, but the small parts contained so much depth and richness. I wanted to memorialize all this knowledge before his memory left him or, even worse, before he died in prison.

I told him I wanted to write it all down and put something together to share with his family. I wanted to let them know the impact he was making from within the prison walls. The world needed to see that there were beautiful souls in prison regardless of their past. He agreed, and we scheduled for the following week. I was so excited.

It was also during the last 150 days that I had to figure out how I would get home without imposing on my family's schedule. I looked into train and bus schedules, and I started researching and plotting my way home. But the more I looked, the more I realized that I wanted to fly home. I wanted to experience flying again; it had been over twenty years since I had stepped foot into a plane. Yet, everyone around me told me that there was no way TSA was going to let me on a flight without proper identification. My family at home, close friends inside, and the prison staff all told me that TSA would make my life horrible if I tried to board a flight. I felt that I could go to TSA and explain it to them, yet everyone insisted that there was no way I could convince them. My own brother told me, "Dude, you don't know how much the world has changed out here since 9/11. You can't just walk up to people and talk to them and change their minds."

I felt confused and unsure, yet the adventurous part of me wanted to experience getting on a flight. Plus, I felt a little indignant that my brother had said I could not change people's minds. I had been helping to change people's hearts and minds for these last few years at Solano, so why could I not do the same in the outside world? Prison was only a location, so even if I left this place and went to another, I felt I could still change people's minds.

In my journal, I told myself that just because I had been away for over sixteen years to never take at face value if someone told me I did not know anything. Part of me felt it was a good thing I didn't know anything about the outside world. My perspective was not limited by the bad experiences of everyday life, and I could view it all with an untarnished lens.

One evening before I was paroled, I was sitting in a circle of about eight of us in our Bible study group, including Robert. Our Bibles sat on our laps, and we had finished reciting the rosary. We checked in with each other by sharing what was going on in our life at that moment. For some reason, the men decided that was the night to have an intervention with me. When I started talking about getting on the flight and clearing TSA, a couple of the guys snickered. I pushed the annoyance away, but it lingered right below the surface.

"Why do you want to put yourself through this? They are going to take you into a holding cell and strip you down, like they do here," Robert stated. The others mumbled in agreement, and I felt everyone was teaming up against me, with Robert the main culprit. After I had been found suitable, some of my closest friends had begun to treat me like an outcast, and it hurt that Robert was one of them. The ugly, contemptuous part of me attacked back in disdain. *None of you fools can be found suitable at the parole board, yet you try to tell me how to get on a plane?*

I pushed the thoughts away as well as I could and squeezed my wrist.

"Guys, why is everyone so against me going to the airport? Let's say the worst-case scenario happens: they take me into a holding cell and strip me down, and then turn me away. What can they do to me that I have never experienced? I guarantee you, I will *still* be the happiest person in that airport no matter what happens! Don't you all see?" I felt the familiar bubbling of my ego rising again, but instead of pushing it away this time, I allowed it to get the best of me. I blurted out, "Plus, I think TSA is going to let me through." The men groaned, and I regretted the words as they left my mouth.

On the day that Robert and I had agreed to sit down and begin our process of taking down his story, he told me he felt a little ill, so we rescheduled for the following week. The following week became another, and the next thing I knew, a month had already passed and Robert still had not sat down with me yet. I felt betrayed and hurt because Robert had been avoiding me. I knew there were issues of being able to say goodbye to me, but I also knew there was much more than that. Robert was his best self inside our workshops. But he was a broken man who had many of his own demons to slay.

One evening, he sat at a table helping one of the other men prepare for an upcoming GED test. They finished, and Robert smiled at me as I came up. I waited until the other man left, and sat down across from Robert.

"I have a gift for you, Robert," I began.

Robert sat up straight and looked at me from behind his smoked glasses.

Inside our workshops, during debriefings, we gave each other feedback on what to improve on, and many of the facilitators called it constructive criticism. At first when I had begun facilitating, I was uncomfortable when it came time to receive feedback. I noticed I only liked to hear the things that I did well but felt quite uneasy and anxious when there were things pointed out that I needed to improve on. But like my NPR radio interview, I learned never to explain and started to realize that feedback was such a gift for me, especially if I embraced it in that spirit. We then coined a term, *gift giving*, and during our debriefings, we prefaced our feedback with "I have a gift for you."

The table felt cold as I leaned my elbows on it. "About a month ago, we were sitting at this table, and I brought up to you about sitting down and hearing your story. You agreed to share it with me. Yet, these last few weeks it seems every time I try to get you to sit down, you tell me you are sick or have some other obligation."

Robert began rubbing the tops of his thighs in a circular motion. He always did that when he was nervous. "I know. I have been meaning to get to it. But then I have to help this person with his GED or that one with something else. I have been so busy helping these other guys." He began to ramble on with other excuses, all the while still rubbing his thighs. "Plus, this is not going to be easy for me."

"So my gift for you, Robert, is it feels to me like you are filling up your time to help others so that you can avoid sitting down with me." I held up my hand before he could respond, and continued. "I understand sitting down and sharing with me is not going to be easy for you. Yet, don't you realize that this will be healing for both you and your family? You have done so much good in here, but what is your legacy if you don't finally face your demons? Robert, I only have 120 days left here and then it will be goodbye." I pushed back the urge to tear up and simply stated, "I would also like to hear your story."

He stayed solemn behind his dark glasses and finally nodded. "OK, let me get some notes out I have been meaning to share with you, and we can begin this next week." He shifted in his seat and then stood up. Even behind his glasses, he would not look me in the eye. The words sounded good, but at that moment, I knew Robert would never sit down with me again. His story would die with him in prison.

My last days at Solano were some of the most heartbreaking for me. In conversations with my friends, sometimes I felt I was outside of my own body and viewing it all from above. There would be uncomfortable silences when I knew that this might be one of the last times I would ever talk to them again. I started to feel guilty that I was going to be released; there were much more deserving men who would die in prison. Even though I knew that I provided hope for those around me, I still felt conflicted inside. My intentions each day were to be present with each man I came across on the yard. I was going home, to freedom, to the "real world," as we called it, yet I felt a deep sense of loss because I knew I would in essence be dying to everyone else in here.

I still needed to plan how I would get past TSA and onto my flight. At that time, I worked as the captain's clerk in the program office and knew how the prison processed the releases each day. Each parolee was able to receive a box from home that had their dress-out clothing. My day would come soon. One morning, I noticed the correctional officer asking the group of men paroling that day for their prison IDs. The prison IDs were plastic cards containing our mug shots and prison numbers. Across the top were the bolded words *California Department of Corrections*. It had always been prison policy to take the prison IDs from each person as they were released; I had just never paid attention to this process.

That day, I decided I needed my prison ID to bolster my story to TSA that I was just released from prison. I made a conscious choice and lied to my supervisor by telling him I lost my ID. He filled out a pass and sent me downstairs to take a picture so they could issue me a new one. It was against the prison rules to have more than one ID, and it would be grounds for a write-up. The stakes were much higher now that I was found suitable. Any type of write-up meant that my date would be taken from me and I would be denied parole for several years. After they issued me my new ID, I went back to the office where I worked and pulled out one of the drawers. I got some masking tape and affixed my ID to the bottom side of the drawer, then slid it closed. I did not tell my coworker or anyone else what I had done. It stayed there until the night before I was due to be released, and I brought it back with me. The next morning during the processing of my release, I kept one ID and gave one to the correctional officer when he asked for it.

A few hours later, I walked into the ground floor of Sacramento airport and stood there for a minute. I was released that morning, but I still had not cleared TSA. It was a bright, sunny day, and there was so much color in all the world around me. The air even smelled fresher on this side of the fence. The only thing I had on me was my expired driver's license, prison ID, and the guitar that had kept me company since my first board denial, held inside a guitar case that had backpack straps. Less than three hours ago, I was still doing a life sentence in prison, and now, I was going to try to get on a flight to Long Beach. I had said most of my goodbyes the night before. There were a few men who got up at dawn to see me off when they called for my release. Robert was nowhere to be seen.

Even though I was released, I had a different set of problems to overcome. Family, friends, and even prison staff had told me there was no way TSA was going to clear me on a flight without proper identification, and I started questioning my own stubbornness.

When I arrived at the airport, the first thing that struck me as odd were these touch-screen kiosks that said "Self-Service Check-In." I looked around until I saw the kiosk for JetBlue, went up, and started pressing away on the screen. Pretty self-explanatory, and then it asked me for my boarding pass code. I typed it in; the night before, I had called home and wrote it down on a piece of paper. A boarding pass printed out with my name, birth date, flight number, and destination. I followed the signs to the TSA clearance area, which had agents everywhere in dark blue uniforms. Irrationally, it felt to me like everyone knew I had just stepped out of prison. I definitely did not want to talk to anyone yet. Instead, I stood and watched for a minute and figured out what to do: walk up to the nearest agent, show boarding pass and ID. My nerves began to get the best of me, but I mustered up the courage and walked up to the booth. The TSA agent who greeted me looked about nineteen years old at the most. I handed him my boarding pass and expired driver's license. He paused and looked a little puzzled. "Sir, this ID looks expired. I have never seen this ID before. Do you have a valid ID?"

This guy was still wearing diapers when I had that ID! I reached into my pocket and pulled out my prison ID and handed it to him. "Hey, I was just released from prison today after sixteen years, and this is the only ID I have." I flashed him a charming smile, hoping it would help.

Diaper boy did not smile back but instead handed me back my IDs and said, "Please step over here, sir."

Sir? Am I that old now? I thought to myself. I stood off to the side and continued to look around. In the background, I could see people taking off shoes and belts and putting them on gray plastic bins that were then placed on a conveyor belt. A couple of passengers who were waiting behind me looked frustrated. I looked down at my driver's license and prison ID. I was no longer the same person who had taken these pictures, I knew that. My family and friends would notice that I had aged, but would any of them recognize how much my own sense of identity had been transformed? *I am much more than the person in these pictures.* Yet, this was the only way the world would accept and identify me.

Within thirty seconds, a middle-aged woman stepped to where I was standing and asked to see my IDs. I disclosed once again that I was just released from prison and gave her a winning smile, too. She looked at me and then looked down at both my IDs. She shuffled the IDs together and then handed them back with my plane ticket. I looked up, and I saw the most genuine, heartwarming smile on her face. "Welcome home," she said. The words brought me to tears, as I finally felt free.

CHAPTER 15

UNHEARD VOICES

PRESIDING COMMISSIONER: OK. So as you look back on it now, what would you describe as the principle of motives for the shooting? Why? Why'd you do it?

INMATE HUYNH: Gang retaliation. My sense of anger at the world, me fulfilling the part in me to still be recognized—I'm not recognized in this part of my life, but here I'll be recognized in this part of my life. This part of my life does not accept me in the world, but I'll gain it over here. I'm ashamed to say that that's what it was.

PRESIDING COMMISSIONER: OK. So need for recognition, especially since you felt that rejection from Gallup?

INMATE HUYNH: Yes.

PRESIDING COMMISSIONER: Can you just tell us what it is, if anything, that you could point to that would be an indicator of your attempts to alleviate pain and suffering of the victims in your crime?

INMATE HUYNH: You know, fi st I want to say that no matter what I do, I don't think I can alleviate their suffering. There's things I can do in some small way. Recently, I spoke at a Victim's Voice impact, and there were crime victims there and I shared my story. Crime victim women came up to me and they tell me that my words provided healing for them. And that really opened my eyes. I might not be able to directly make any type of amends to Ms. Julie Nguyen. I can never do anything to bring back Mr. Minh Nguyen, but the small things I can do to share my message and to provide some type of healing for somebody else, that's how I believe I can give back. I can give back when I facilitate the workshops and I share myself, my story with other men. There's numerous ways I can give back in small ways, but I don't think—the scale is never going to be righted. I say that knowing full well that is a debt that I owe for the rest of my life and that I'm going to continue with this.

I have been home now about three and a half years, and part of the return home has been more wonderful than I could have imagined. Every Sunday, my mom and I go to Mass, and after, we grab lunch together. We refer to it as our Sunday lunch date. I am absolutely happy in her presence. We are no longer sitting inside a crowded visiting room with small tables and eating vending machine food. I no longer see the look of hopelessness on my mother's face, the same look of hopelessness that was on every mother's face in those visiting rooms.

I created my first company six months after parole. I'm working at an organization where I can help other men and women with criminal histories to create their own companies, too. I have been able to meet some amazing human beings out here, many of whom I can call friends.

But not everything has been amazing. I still face my own challenges. In prison, I had learned to communicate and connect with other men in meaningful ways. Many of us were on the same page about personal development and effective communication. Out here, I have struggled to receive and achieve that same level of respect, dignity, and thoughtfulness when it comes to communication. I look back over my life and realize about twenty-two years of it has been behind bars. In that time, though, I have evolved and become more mindful in my words. I understand today how powerful words are, and I can either say things to build people up or say things to tear them down.

Out here, though, the vast majority of people have not had the opportunity to do much self-examination, and words have felt harsh, critical, and judgmental. It's frustrating when I try to speak and communicate the way I had practiced inside and realize that my words are not landing well, or at all, with the person I am speaking to.

There is a small community of former lifers out here. I am part of a monthly support group where we still gather and share our perspectives and achievements. There is a saying in our community that is widely accepted when we talk about difficulties out here. The men always like to recite, "My worst day out here is better than my best day in there." But I have come to believe this is a lie. Some of my most beautiful days were when I was in prison, where I was present with my community. There was a shared purpose and meaning in our existence. I feel we are doing ourselves a disservice when we cannot admit that there are actually some things we miss about prison. For example, I miss being able to play a pickup game of handball or get a group of guys together on the yard to throw the football. I miss walking counterclockwise on the track in deep conversation with someone. I miss having a lot of free time on my hands to read or play the guitar. I miss cooking and eating together with a bunch of friends. I miss the community of lifers that I left behind.

Today, I still live with the stigma of being someone who was incarcerated. In prison, it was easy to say that I was in for murder. Out here, the stain hovers over anyone who has come home, trying to adjust. One of the first places my brother and his wife took me when I got out was their yoga studio. As we walked in, they told me I should not let anyone know I was released from prison. As they put it, nobody would understand. Conversations with people in my new world were awkward.

I bought a house last year in a beautiful and peaceful gated community. My neighbors have no idea of my past, and although they all know I work in the reentry space, I fear their judgment if they were to ever know I was incarcerated. I can picture them shunning me or, worse yet, become fearful for their kids because I was in prison for murder. I have moved my mother home, and her friends and coworkers have come by. She also never told them where I had been all these years. I see the anxiousness in her face when they inevitably ask me about what type of work I do or what I was up to before I "moved" back to Southern California. Although I would love to, I do not disclose the whole truth. Sometimes I feel like I have betrayed the men I left behind because I am hiding my past. I know it is unfair, but I judge myself for not being completely honest with my true self and fearing judgment from others.

In prison, I was able to attain a tremendous amount of intimacy through the shared struggle and brotherhood of the men in there. We learned to support and listen to each other. I feel like I am not completely accepted out here. In coming home, I realize I struggle with emotional vulnerability when it comes to women and relationships. I believed it when women I dated told me I did not know better because of my prison experience. I have gotten involved with unhealthy relationships that were not in alignment with where I wanted to go in my life. It was only to fill that loneliness that I struggle with inside. Some days, I feel alone and disconnected, and alcohol also numbs that void for me. I know it is an unhealthy coping habit, yet I still choose to fill that emptiness with liquor. Two years after parole, I was arrested for driving under the influence of alcohol. I continue to slip and fail, but one thing I learned from prison was to dust myself off and get back up.

Despite all these challenges, I still move forward.

There is still something that weighs heavy on my heart, though. Back in 2011, when I started to grasp what remorse was, I wrote a letter to the mother of the man I killed, Mrs. Julie Nguyen. At first, when I started to put the letter together, it was three to four pages long with all these eloquent-sounding words. In looking it over, though, I realized I wrote to impress others and not to connect with her. In the letter, I explained why I did what I did. But what did it really matter? I mean, what could I say to the mother of the man I had killed? If I had been killed that night, what could someone have said to my own mother to alleviate her pain?

I realized there was nothing I could say. But I wanted to say something. I needed to say something. I chopped up the letter, cutting it down to the bare essentials. I was content with it, and it held for me the essence of what I wanted to say. Then I sent it off to the Office of Victims Services, an organization that would forward the letter to her. Several months later, the original letter was sent back to my central file, which meant she never registered with them and would never receive my letter.

My friends on the yard informed me this was good news.

Because she had never registered with the Office of Victims Services, she would not show up at my board hearing. A prisoner's chance of being granted parole was always slim, but it disappeared when a victim attended. Yet, I was conflicted. I felt guilty for hoping I might go home with my own mother. I was relieved that I would not have to apologize to her face-to-face. But I was also ashamed that none of these feelings were about her and her pain.

I still have that letter and would like to share it because she never received it.

> November 5, 2011
>
> Dear Mrs. Julie Nguyen,
>
> I want you to know I am truly sorry for taking your son's life. I am sorry for forever tainting the way you may see the world and taking the joy out of it. I pray that in some small way my words could provide some measure of healing for you.
>
> I want you to know that I am not the same person that committed this violent and senseless act and am living a life from here on out to honor the man whom I will be forever paying my penance for, your son, Minh Nguyen.

I will never hear her pain, but I will always carry my own.

ACKNOWLEDGMENTS

Dad, I still miss you to this day. Fuck cancer. I promise to take care of Mom until you are reunited with her.

Mom, you are the constant rock in my life. I am so grateful to be near you, and I still enjoy listening to you talk about anything and everything. Tuan, you should have been the older brother. Trinh, my little sis, I am so proud of the woman you have become. Co Hue, your letters were such nourishment for my starved soul when I needed them most. Aileen, thank you for loving me like a brother all those years. Joey, thank you for safeguarding my journals. My precious niece, Alyssa Jade Huynh, I hope you read this and understand one day.

To the ones we lost to a life of dust—Wray, Leesh, and Imad, rest in peace wherever you are at. Smurfette, karaoke has never been the same without you.

Sarah Vincent, you knew God had a plan for me. Thanks for giving me the guitar. Donnie Douglas, you helped me find myself. The homies Peter Nguyen and "Big Rick" Benton, you guys rode with me at my worst and stood by me when I was trying to be my best. Phillip "Ralphie" Hernandez, the best accountability partner and bunky.

Jayson Gaignard, thanks for inviting me to join the MMT community. What an amazing group of human beings! Philip McKernan, for telling me that I belonged. Tucker Max, for telling me to shut the fuck up and to just bring my ass out to Austin.

Diana Chu and Tatiana Becker, thanks for giving me feedback and words of encouragement along the way. Dorothy and Kathy Do, thank you for being such amazing listeners. Julie Jackson-Forsberg, only you and I know how your subtle fingerprints helped with my book.

My Soledad brothers, Andrew Nguyen, Frank Lee and Minh Ngo, we made it.

To all my brothers still left behind, particularly Bobby and Robert, I hope you have found your freedom in some small way.

And finally, Our Father up above, who provides the constant light to help us find the way back home.

ABOUT THE AUTHOR

QUAN HUYNH has been described as a mighty warrior, a magician, and a mountain of goodness. He is the post-release program manager for Defy Ventures, a nonprofit helping those with a criminal past transform their lives through the journey of entrepreneurship.

After spending twenty-two years in and out of correctional institutions, Quan was paroled from a life sentence in 2015 and created his first company six months later. The following year, he received the Peace Fellowship Award for his work with the Alternatives to Violence Project. Quan has been featured in *Entrepreneur*, PBS Newshour, Talks at Google, and numerous other publications and podcasts.

Find out more about Quan at www.quanxhuynh.com

To contact Quan, write to him at 3550 Wilshire Blvd, Ste 1550, Los Angeles, CA 90010

2008—Solano State Prison. Left to right: my dormmate, me.

2009—Solano State Prison. Taken in the dorm. Left to right: me and my dormmates.

1988—My father's funeral. Left to right: paternal grandmother, aunt, sister, mom, brother, me.

1988—My father's funeral. My brother, me. We wear the white mourning cloths to signify immediate family members of the deceased.

1988—My father's funeral. In our tradition, the first-born son (me) leads the pallbearers with his photo.

1988—At my father's gravesite. My brother, me before I started high school.

1998—Las Vegas, 6 months before the murder.

1988—8th grade graduation, 6 weeks after my father's death, my mother and me.

1976—San Francisco, California. Brother, mom, me.

1979—Provo, Utah, at my uncle's wedding. Clockwise, left to right: My sister, great-uncle, father, mother, brother, and me.

1981—Lake Tahoe vacation, before my father was diagnosed with leukemia. Left to right: Mom, brother, sister, me.

1973—My father as a young lieutenant in the City of Hue, Vietnam.

1974—Me as a newborn with my father in Da Lat, Vietnam.

2007—Solano State Prison

1981—Lake Tahoe vacation, before my father was diagnosed with leukemia. Me, brother, sister.

1997—From left to right: me, my brother, sister, and mom after I paroled my third time from the California Youth Authority.

2003—Donovan State Prison

1986—Me, in the Budweiser hat. At this time I was going to the creative writing school at the University of California, Irvine.

2019 Avenal State Prison

2018 California Institute for Women

2018 California Institute for Women

2019 Kern Valley State Prison

2017 Security Housing Unit at Pelican Bay State Prison

2019 Kern Valley State Prison

Made in the USA
Middletown, DE
07 September 2021